W9-BMN-684

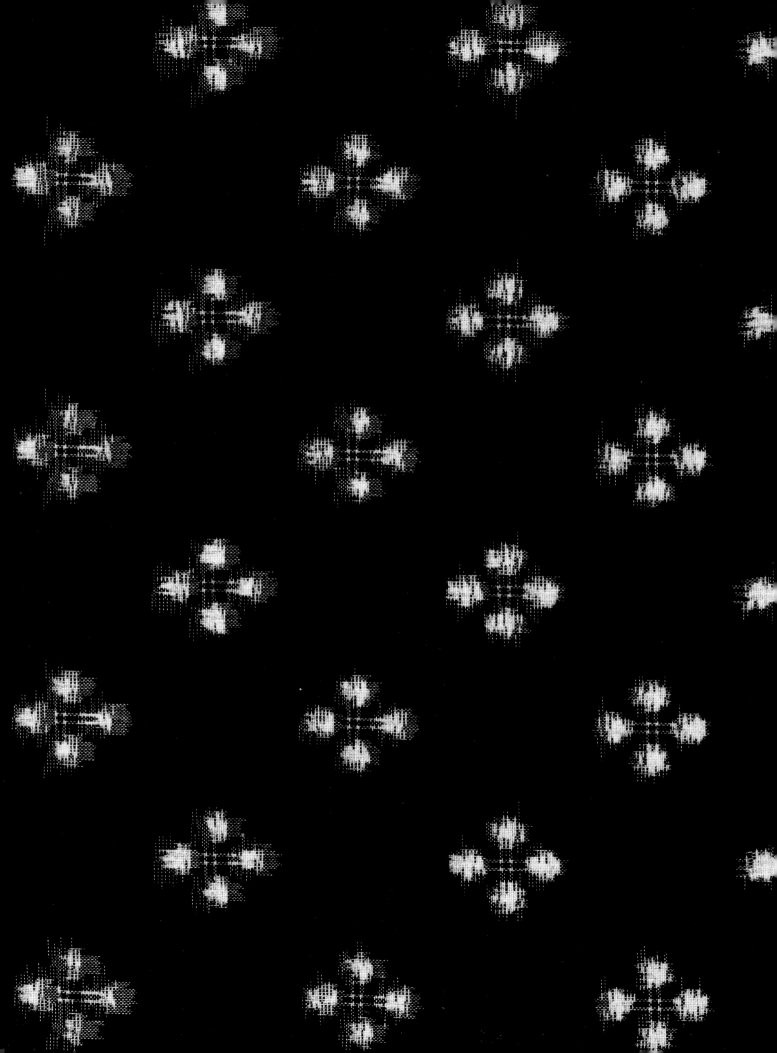

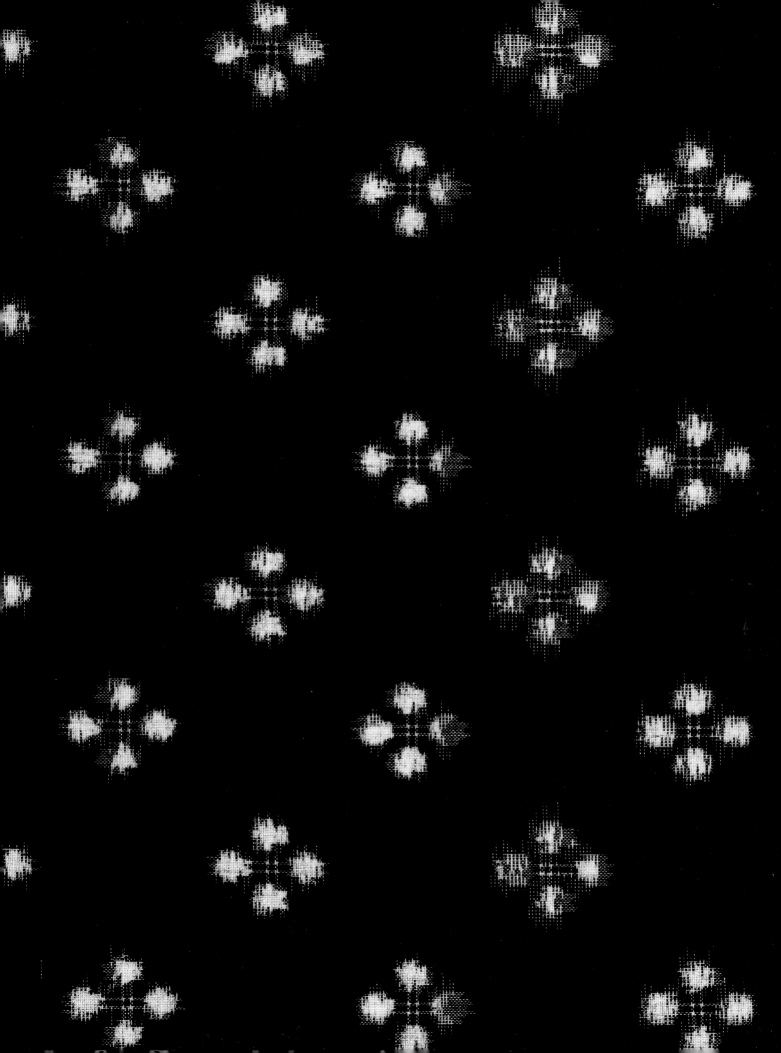

I wish to dedicate this book to
the memory of Michael Kile
for his inspiration, guidance, and
constant encouragement.

東キルト西

KUMIKO SUDO

EAST
QUILTS
WEST

THE QUILT DIGEST PRESS

Copyright © 1992 by Kumiko Sudo.
All rights reserved.

No part of this publication may be reproduced, stored in a retrieval system,
or transmitted in any form or by any means, electronic, mechanical, photo-
copying, recording, or otherwise, without prior written permission of the
copyright owner.

Published in the United States of America by The Quilt Digest Press.

Editorial and production direction by Bill Folk.
Production management by James Nelson.
Cover copy by Sharon Gilbert.
Editing by Nancy Bruning.
Copy editing by Janet Reed.
Book and cover design by Kajun Graphics, San Francisco.
Illustrations by Marcía McGetrick.
Technical editing and assembly diagrams by Kandy Petersen.
Photography by Sharon Risedorph, San Francisco.
Typographical composition by DC Typography, San Francisco.
Printing by Nissha Printing Company Ltd., Kyoto, Japan.
Color separations by the printer.

*The author thanks Hoffman California Fabrics, Momen House Fabrics,
and RJR Fashion Fabrics for their support.*

First Printing

Library of Congress Cataloging-in-Publication Data

Sudō, Kumiko.
        East quilts west / by Kumiko Sudō
                p.   cm.
        ISBN 0-913327-37-9
        1. Sudō, Kumiko — Themes, motives.   2. Quilts — Japan
        — History — 20th century.   3. Quilts — United States —
        History — 20th century.
        I. Title.
        NK9198.S8A4   1992
        746.3'92 — dc20   92-24027
                                                            CIP

The Quilt Digest Press
P.O. Box 1331
Gualala, California 95445

This book is about spirit.

It was born out of the inspired vision of Michael Kile, a special publisher, which he shared with Kumiko Sudo, a unique artist. The result is a lively interplay between the Eastern sensibilities of the artist's design brilliance and Western approaches to quilt designs and techniques.

East Quilts West is a hybrid: both fine art and how-to presentation of fifty-three original block designs and eight complete quilts created for quiltmakers, designers, and fine artists. In these pages, we invite you to explore the surprising approaches to using designs, fabrics, and patterns that are sure to entice and excite.

Through Kumiko Sudo's spirit-infused work, Michael's legacy of excellence, beauty, and commitment to "Simply the Best" lives on. It will also continue through you, as the artist's work inspires you to create your own unique quilts that will further serve as testaments to the spirit of this collaboration.

The Quilt Digest Press
Gualala, California
October 1992

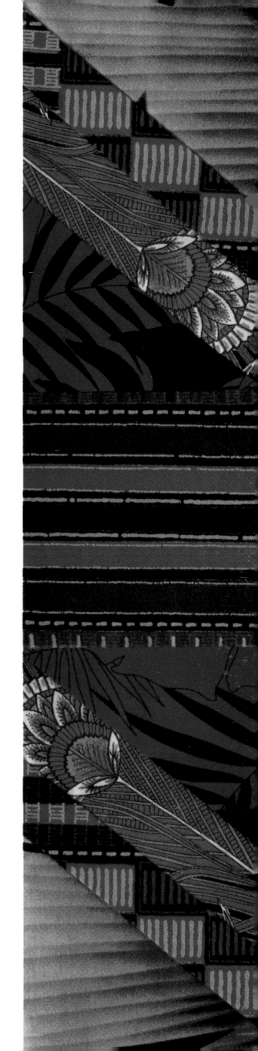

CONTENTS

8 *Introduction: A Conversation with Kumiko Sudo*

19 *How to Use This Book*

Blocks and Quilts

24 HINAMATSURI
25 HIKIDASHI
26 SAKURA
27 KAMON ✿
32 HOKUSAI
33 FUNADE
34 RADIO CITY MUSIC HALL
35 SHOP WINDOWS
36 CHO NO MAI
37 JESTER
38 HIZASHI
39 QUATTROCENTO ✿
44 MATSUKASA
45 KANZASHI
46 DOWNTOWN
47 FUYUDORI
48 MORNING GLORY
49 OPERA HOUSE
50 EGYPTIAN FAN
51 TOPKAPI ✿
56 PLANETARIUM
57 ANTIQUE RADIO
58 INDY 500
59 PROPELLERS
60 IRORI
61 MATSURI
62 CLEOPATRA

63 TROPICAL GARDEN ✿
68 SAFARI
69 MIRROR BALL
70 UCHIWA TO SENSU
71 KASUMI
72 PHONOGRAPH
73 SPACE CENTER ✿
78 EGYPTIAN
79 PERGOLA
80 CADILLAC
81 CHARLESTON
82 HUNTING PARTY
83 ROSE GARDEN ✿
88 AQUARIUM
89 CAROUSEL
90 CAMELLIA
91 KABUKI
92 ELECTRIC FAN
93 SCOTTISH THISTLE ✿
98 BRILLIANT CUT
99 O-SHOGATSU
100 WAYWARD WIND
101 ROMANESQUE ✿
106 GENROKU
107 IKEGAKI
108 BACKYARD

111 *Templates*

197 *Lesson Plans*

✿ *Instructions for full quilts follow these block pages*

▲ ME AT ABOUT NINE YEARS OLD, WEARING ONE OF THE SILK KIMONOS MY MOTHER MADE FOR SPECIAL OCCASIONS.

► (FACING PAGE) MY FATHER WAS A YOUNG MAN OF NINE-TEEN OR TWENTY AND HAD JUST BEGUN HIS CAREER IN PHOTOGRAPHY WHEN THIS PHOTOGRAPH WAS TAKEN.

INTRODUCTION

A Conversation with Kumiko Sudo

Kumiko Sudo agrees with painter Georgia O'Keeffe who once wrote, "colors and shapes make a more definite statement than words." Kumiko's designs stand on their own; however, the combination of her colors, shapes, and words presents a richer, deeper statement. With this thought in mind, the following conversation with Kumiko Sudo will add to your understanding and appreciation of her work.

When did your interest in quilt designing begin?

I was only five years old when I began to show an interest in fabrics and colors. Perhaps my early interest was in part due to my father who was a professional photographer. Color film was not yet available, so for custom orders he would brush pigments on the individual photographs. I was usually beside him watching the entire process with great curiosity. My father was very innovative and manipulated various techniques of his own to create unusual products. For instance, he would cut shapes such as umbrellas or flowers from paper and incorporate them into the photograph; he would use multiple exposures or print multiple negatives; he would use an airbrush to change the appearance of the original clothes. He was so eager to improve his skill he even rebuilt and modified his own equipment; he obtained more than one hundred patents for various ideas.

On July 7, we celebrate the Tanabata Festival. On this day you could most clearly see the stars that represent two lovers in a Chinese folktale, who only saw each other once a year. For this holiday, my father, who had great manual dexterity, would cleverly manipulate scissors and colored paper to create beautiful ornaments. We would hang them from bamboo branches from which also hung various cards written with best wishes and hopes for the future by each member of the family.

CROSS-CULTURAL QUILTING

Kumiko Sudo's work has been described as a masterful combination of the traditional American quilt construction methods of piecing, layering, and appliqué, with the traditional Japanese stitching technique of sashiko. *Although the way she expresses herself through these techniques is of course unique, and contemporary quilt making is comparatively new in Japan, all these techniques have been used for centuries. And the arts and crafts of the East and West have been influencing each other for quite some time.*

QUILTING, *for example, holds together the layers of the traditional futon, which the Japanese use as both mattress and bed cover. Futons of the past were beautifully decorative and made either of silk (for the rich) or indigo-dyed and patterned cotton. Centuries ago the Chinese were among many Eastern peoples who wore quilted armor as protection against arrows and swords and quilted clothing as protection against the cold. It is believed that Crusaders in the eleventh century brought the idea of quilted garments to Europe, and that these eventually led to quilted bed covers.*

PATCHWORK *in Japan seems to have practical, religious, and aesthetic origins that interweave with and reinforce one another. On the practical side, there was the economic necessity of preserving and recycling precious fabrics, which at times were even used as currency to pay tribute to emperors and to reward good service. This tradition prevailed well into the 1800s because the Japanese government enforced a policy of national seclusion. In an effort to curtail Western influence, Japan was sealed off from the rest of the world. Trade with other nations ceased, and as a result fabrics were hoarded.*

According to Shinto, the indigenous religion in Japan, all things, including cloth, have a spirit. Historically the Japanese have revered and loved cloth, considering it a treasure to be cherished. Prolonging the life of an old fabric, such as through salvaging scraps to use in patchwork, came to be a spiritual exercise. To this day, transforming scraps into something that is useful and artistic exemplifies the Japanese idea of beauty. Buddhism, too, which arrived in Japan in the sixth century, encouraged the craft of patchwork. Buddhist monks took a vow of poverty and wore patched robes. The geometric, orderly design of the patches in Buddhist robes supposedly symbolized the patterns of the rice paddies in Buddha's native India. Patchwork cloths are still considered to be fine offerings in Buddhist temples.

Was your mother an early influence?

Oh, yes. I remember the time we each kept pictorial journals, which we would exchange. I was nine years old and temporarily living with my aunt in Kamakura, a beautiful resort city not far from Tokyo. Once a month my mother came to see me with her journal full of collages accompanied by short stories or verses. The collages were made of printed food labels from glass jars, tin cans, and packages. She cut out cherries, strawberries, and sometimes cows with wreaths around their necks and assembled them artfully on colored papers. These were always able to console my lonely heart. While I was waiting on

the hillside under the sun, my mother would suddenly appear from the dark tunnel connecting the road to the train station; I could not wait to jump up and show her my own pictorial journal. Without waiting to arrive at my aunt's house, we shared our journals along the narrow path leading to the house on the hill where I was living.

It seems your quilt designs and your writings continue the idea of the journal.

Yes, I draw inspiration from my everyday life, and the stories I created to accompany the quilt designs include pieces of my culture, my past, and my present. And, I am still very fond of fabrics printed with strawberries and cherries, which bring back both the happiness and the sorrow of my childhood memories.

■ 11 ■

◄ (FACING PAGE) AN EXAMPLE OF MY FATHER'S INNOVATIVE PHOTOGRAPHY TECHNIQUES. HE SUPERIMPOSED THE IMAGE OF MY OLDER SISTER WITH IMAGES OF THE SILK UMBRELLAS MY SISTERS USED DURING DANCE PERFORMANCES.

▲ MY MOTHER USED FABRIC FROM ONE OF HER KIMONOS TO MAKE THIS ONE FOR MY OLDEST SISTER, WHICH WAS PASSED ON TO MY OTHER SISTER AND THEN TO ME.

▼ AN EARLY PHOTOGRAPH OF ME WEARING A BRIGHTLY COLORED SILK KIMONO. WHEN I BECAME OLDER, THIS KIMONO WAS USED IN MAKING FAMILY COMFORTERS.

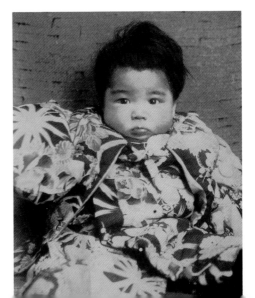

How did you switch from cutting out paper pictures to working with fabrics?

My mother was indirectly responsible. She was very well versed in literature and wanted to be a writer, but she ended up as an instructor in flower arrangement and the tea ceremony. She was also a very good dressmaker and knitter and created her own designs. I was the envy of other pupils because I was always dressed in vogue! When my mother opened two dressmaking and fabric shops it gave me the opportunity to create decorative items myself, and I asked her to put them on display. Customers liked the things I made and I became involved with the business. I entered a well-known designers' school in Tokyo and also took lessons from a New Yorker in millinery. I met wonderful artists who owned galleries and boutiques in the Ginza, Tokyo and they interested me in the world of fine art. I

▲ ANOTHER KIMONO MY MOTHER MADE FOR MY SISTERS AND ME USING FABRIC SALVAGED FROM HER OWN KIMONO.

▶ (FACING PAGE) MY FATHER TOOK THIS PHOTOGRAPH OF MY MOTHER BEFORE THEY WERE MARRIED. SHE HAD JUST ARRIVED IN TOKYO AND WAS STUDYING WRITING AT THE TIME.

▼ THE LINING OF THIS KIMONO HAS BEEN TIE-DYED USING THE *SHIBORI* TECHNIQUE; THE FABRIC WAS MY GRANDMOTHER'S AND IS ALMOST ONE HUNDRED YEARS OLD.

APPLIQUÉ AND EMBROIDERY *were less common than quilting and patchwork because the Japanese were so adept at decorating cloth with stencil and resist-dyeing. Traditionally, the aboriginal race called the Ainu were the appliquérs of Japan. In the middle of the eighteenth century, this island people developed a kind of appliqué technique using cotton cloth. The Ainu turned the wonderfully intricate symmetrical designs used in their wood carvings into cloth patterns, which they appliquéd onto their elm-bark fiber clothing. Some of their designs resemble the Hawaiian style of appliqué. As was the case with patchwork, this practical and decorative art reflected religious beliefs. Appliqué was considered to be a "spiritual armor," and the Ainu believed that the more intricate the design, the more protection it provided the wearer against evil spirits.*

SASHIKO *is a type of decorative stitching that is a hybrid of embroidery and quilting.* Sashiko *means "little stabs" and was originally a simple running stitch used to repair and strengthen fabrics. The stitching was used to hold together several layers of the loose and flimsy cloth available at the time. The arrival of sturdier cotton cloth freed women to be more inventive with their stitchery and* sashiko *designs became more decorative. Today,* sashiko *is still used to impart quilts with wonderful textures.*

traveled extensively all over the world visiting museums and learned to appreciate paintings and sculptures. Finally my journey ended when I encountered antique quilts in Palo Alto, California. At last I found my ultimate direction as a life work.

How was it that your experience in Palo Alto became such a big turning point for you?

It was the summer of 1970. In Palo Alto I came across an antique wedding ring quilt at one of the antique shops near Stanford University. I perceived the work as a layman and felt the necessity of educating myself in the fundamentals of the craft to comprehend the work fully. So I started to study quilts, their historical background, their techniques, and the stories behind them.

Do you have a quilting tradition in your family?

Looking back at my childhood, though nobody called them quilts, I certainly witnessed similar works in my house and those of my relatives: boldly patched comforters, cushions, and woolen vests.

What excites you most about quilting: the designing or the sewing and quilting?

Since my work is not merely a graphic design but really a narrative with a story element, it is impossible to separate one from the other. I emphasize the creation of emotional impact or inspiration on the flat surfaces. When I attain the realization of those elements in my work, then — and only then — do I enjoy a certain degree of satisfaction and pleasure.

How do you create a quilt design? Do the fabrics inspire you, or do you start with a design and then find the fabric?

I often visit fabric stores to examine the latest prints and shades. It is quite exciting to find new fabrics, but I do not necessarily buy them to use immediately. Rather, I keep them for "reference" and stockpile them for future designs. Occasionally certain fabrics with beautiful colors and delightful prints inspire me to create new designs, but most of the time developing a design is a very independent task. Under certain conditions it comes to me quite readily and at other times I must struggle to transform a wisp of an idea into reality. Once I have completed drafting the design, I shift my entire concentration and effort toward finding the right piece of fabric to fill the hundreds of blanks in various shapes and sizes. The shortcomings of the design itself can be modified by manipulating fabrics, but inferior color arrangements cannot be corrected later on.

▲ THIS PHOTOGRAPH OF ME WAS TAKEN BY MY FATHER ON MY FIRST DAY OF SCHOOL. THE BLACK VELVET DRESS I AM WEARING WAS MADE BY MY MOTHER.

▶ (FACING PAGE) WHEN I FIRST STARTED MAKING QUILTS, I USED TRADITIONAL AMERICAN PATCHWORK DESIGNS, SUCH AS THE *CROWN OF THORNS* SHOWN HERE, AND INTERPRETED THEM USING MY OWN FABRIC CHOICES.

Your fabric choices are so unique — what advice about fabric selection would you give other quilters?

I hope people will realize from studying the designs in this book that it is not always necessary to buy the usual quilting fabric with small print designs. If you buy some fabrics with bold or dynamic designs, you will be surprised as to how useful and exciting such printed designs can be. When you see a fabric you really like, it is a good idea to buy at least a yard or so even though you may not have an immediate use for it. In this way you can build a collection of fabrics that gives you the most pleasure and satisfaction. In addition, keeping fabric from clothes that family members have once worn is an old but important tradition for quilters. Incorporating such fabrics really adds to the heart and spirit of one's work and the memories of people and places will always be remembered with fondness and gratitude.

How did you get the idea of blending or mixing Japanese designs, subjects, and sensibilities with American ones?

Ukiyo-e, a vulgar form of art that had only a modest reputation among cultivated Japanese, reached the Western world in the form of wrapping paper. It deeply influenced most artists at that time — especially Monet, Toulouse-Lautrec, and Whistler. To this day, the nineteenth-century masters Hokusai,

YOSEGIRE is a style, a technique, and a phenomenon that resembles the crazy-quilt type of patchwork that was the rage in the United States during the late 1800s. There are Japanese examples of this type of construction dating back hundreds of years. Although developed as a means of preserving precious fabrics, in the last half of the nineteenth century, women used yosegire purely as a fun way to decorate cloth and screens with a variety of colors, shapes, and textures. The random organization of patches eventually became so popular in Japan that it began to be dyed onto fabric, and today it is used to decorate porcelain and papers, too. Decorative Japanese screens displayed in the United States in 1876 are credited with starting the crazy patchwork fad in this country.

Quilts were not the only means of East-West cross-cultural influence. With the opening of Japan, many Western painters showed Japanese influence in their work, including Claude Monet, Toulouse-Lautrec, Vincent van Gogh, and James McNeill Whistler. The story and music from Puccini's Madame Butterfly and Gilbert and Sullivan's Mikado would not exist had the composers not been exposed to Japanese culture.

Hiroshige, and Utamaro remain for most Westerners the supreme Japanese artists. Today, many people including myself find those masterpieces tinted by Ukiyo-e most interesting. If you find some sort of Western influence in my work, it is because I adopt Western theories such as composition, value, and — most importantly — manipulation of printed fabrics the way painters use oil paints to capture movement and depth.

Where do you get the inspiration for your more whimiscal pieces, like the shirts on the clothesline in the block design called Backyard?

No matter how busy I am, I make it a rule to play the piano at least one hour a day to take a break and clear my mind. As I play simple Japanese melodies from my childhood or themes from classical music, I think about how the title of the music was derived or the process of composition, and these thoughts mingle with my past pleasant experiences. I look out at the distant lake between tall fir trees. Often a doe and her fawn are strolling by and birds with red spots on their heads are flying about. I see the moss gracefully hanging from oak trees like green snow. While I observe these things happening around me many ideas come to my mind.

When I am in the city, I often take the opportunity to enjoy the ballet, the opera, or music concerts. Inspiration may come from the noise that an excited audience makes before the orchestra starts. Sometimes, while my eyes are fixed on a prima ballerina leaping in the forest, I find myself comparing her perfection to my own intense concentration while designing my work and become overwhelmed by tears. In such a state of ecstasy and fascination I float into another world; I can clearly visualize new scenes and I often produce new designs.

I have been analyzing how I create new ideas in general and am gradually grasping this fundamental idea: I am a careful observer. I get hints from everywhere — even from characters on TV programs and from spoken words during conversations with friends. I examine every page of all sorts of books and often explore museums with an eye for new designs. I like to go to furniture stores and antique shops. I may derive an interesting idea from the delicate curve of Victorian furniture or the unique form of antique porcelain dolls.

Experts attribute the modern interest in quilt making in both the United States and Japan to an exhibit of antique quilts that toured in the 1970s. The antique fabrics charmed those who saw them and, in the words of one expert, "stirred a memory of a way of life that had seemed destined to be lost forever." She was talking of her Japanese countrywomen, but she might have meant American women as well. American and Japanese quilt designs have evolved over hundreds of years of cross-cultural influence, and now the United States and Japan are the two largest quilt markets in the world.

I never pressure myself to produce an idea — this doesn't work because the idea must come naturally. I usually leave four by six inch note pads in handy places, and every time I come up with an idea, no matter how minimal, I make a sketch and include the date. Later, I go through the thumbnail sketches and transform them into larger forms. Sometimes I combine several sketches in various ways and these combinations result in new, unexpected designs.

Would you categorize your work as American or Japanese; traditional or modern?

At this moment, I do not fit my work into any particular category. Actually I do not wish to be categorized. My designs are just me. I design patterns consisting of shapes that have grace,

▲ AS WITH THE OTHER KIMONOS, MY MOTHER MADE THIS ONE BY HAND FOR ME AND MY SISTERS TO WEAR. I KEEP THESE KIMONOS CAREFULLY STORED IN A CHEST AND TAKE THEM OUT EVERY ONCE IN A WHILE TO LOOK AT THEM AND REMEMBER MY CHILDHOOD.

▼ MY OLDER SISTER AND I IN OUR SUMMER KIMONOS. IN THE BACKGROUND ARE BRANCHES FROM A CHERRY TREE MY FATHER BROUGHT BACK FOR ME FROM A TRIP TO NORTHERN JAPAN.

rhythm, and movement. I use colors to express the variations in light seen at dawn, during the daytime, at sunset, and during the evening to create a feeling of space, depth, and height. I also create another pattern within the pattern by maneuvering printed fabrics to obtain this effect.

In choosing colors, I just follow my intuition or the mood of the day. Spontaneity is very important to my work. Whether I pick up subtle color, or make the color more intense, or introduce strong contrast or less contrast — these all depend on how I react to the individual pattern at the time. I have over two thousand different fabrics. To make the process of choosing fabrics go more smoothly, I have cut a two-inch square of each and put these in color categories such as blue, red, yellow. I arrange them by group, and create a fabric palette, like an oil painter does. By trial and error I find just the right fabric for each shape in the design.

Today, we are surrounded by an abundance of everything, including fabrics. Even with my two thousand fabrics I often encounter problems with finding the right fabrics for the right spot. When Picasso was young and living in poverty, his palette was very limited. Nevertheless he produced many great paintings full of pathos during his Blue and Rose periods. Whenever I think of this, I cannot help but admonish myself for my endless search for fabrics.

What's next for Kumiko Sudo?

Creating the patterns for this book within a limited time was challenging. But I found myself widening my scope, sharpening my inner vision, and venturing into exciting and unfamiliar territories. Now I feel happy and ready to explore new avenues, to express my inner philosophy in different works.

HOW TO USE THIS BOOK

In this book you will find:

EIGHT QUILT DESIGNS including:
- a color photo and diagram of each quilt
- a color photo and diagram of each pattern block
- step-by-step piecing instructions with drawings
- fabric requirements for a variety of quilt sizes
- template patterns for each pattern block
- metric equivalents for all measurements

FORTY-FIVE ADDITIONAL BLOCK DESIGNS including:
- a color photo and diagram of each block
- step-by-step piecing instructions
- template patterns for each block
- metric equivalents for all measurements

In other words, a total of fifty-three new designs to inspire, excite, and delight you.

WHERE TO BEGIN

As you look through its pages, you'll notice that *East Quilts West* is not like other quilting books. The designs and the fabrics are a meeting of Eastern and Western design, color, and culture. We invite you to explore this other culture as fully as you like. As you are reading, why not burn some incense and sip a cup of green tea? Why not find an album of Japanese music to provide more Japanese atmosphere? If you've never had sushi, this may be the perfect time to try it. Why not experiment with origami (the Japanese art of paper folding)? A bit of experience will make it easier for you to follow the origami-like step-by-step drawings that accompany the instructions for the quilts. While these suggestions are not essential, they will help you better understand and enter into the spirit of Kumiko's quilts.

Some of the designs may look puzzling at first, almost off-balance, as if the blocks were cut up and tossed around. The fabric color and pattern combinations are often like nothing we've ever seen before. But as you study them, their own unique beauty, harmony, subtlety, and logic becomes clearer. In the past, Kumiko used silk from old Japanese garments to make quilts. In this book, all the fabrics in the blocks and quilts are contemporary American fabrics. Yet in many cases, the overall effect still reflects a Japanese sensibility. Since the fabrics are available in the United States you can probably duplicate the fabric choices. However, Kumiko feels that color is an individual expression and her choices are for inspiration, not instruction. In Japan, certain colors and design patterns have symbolic meaning, and these are part of her cultural heritage. This history of color makes her approach different from traditional quilting and is, she feels, what gives her quilts their unique character. So, you can make a "Kumiko quilt" or make one that has your own individual imprint on it.

POINTERS ON TECHNIQUE

This book is different not only in design and spirit, but in technical matters too. To ensure successful and pleasurable quilt making, keep these in mind:

■ This book is for people who have at least basic skills in quilt making. If you are new to this craft, you should first familiarize yourself through a book such as *Quilts! Quilts!! Quilts!!!*

■ Advanced quilters should have no problem with any of the fifty-three designs. Eight of the fifty-three blocks also include instructions for making a complete quilt in various sizes. These eight include detailed how-to illustrations that accompany the step-by-step instructions for making the block. Beginners are best advised to start with one of these illustrated blocks to familiarize themselves with Kumiko's methods of sewing. Then you can go on to make other blocks more easily, comfortably, and confidently. Beginning and intermediate quilters will also find it easier to first try blocks with few or no curved seams.

■ Many quilters are skilled at sewing curved seams by machine, but many others prefer to tackle them by hand sewing. Kumiko prefers to use a form of appliqué for curved seams. This technique involves placing a fabric piece, with the seam allowance folded under, on top of the other piece; the fold is placed along the seamline of the lower piece and blind stitched by hand. The word *appliqué* in the instructions means to use this method when curved seams are involved. The term *sew* indicates the traditional method of sewing pieces together, right sides facing, using a running stitch on the wrong side along the seamline. Straight seams are sewn together this way, and you may use hand or machine stitching. Kumiko stitches everything — curved and straight — by hand. Although it's "okay" for others to sew by machine, she feels that the hand is directed not only by the eye, but also by the heart. Further, for Kumiko the machine puts a distance between her and the work.

■ The fabric needed charts may seem to specify an overly large amount of fabric in some cases. This is because curved pieces take up more space and result in more wasted fabric. In addition, the amounts listed are on the generous side because it is far better to have a bit too much fabric than a bit too little.

■ The fabric needed amounts for borders on the quilts are figured without piecing if they are over 2″ (5 cm) wide. Narrower borders are figured to be pieced, to save fabric. Of course, the decision to piece or not to piece is up to you. Sometimes the border is of one of the fabrics that appear in the block; in this case, you may want to use the waste fabric from the border to make the block pieces. Notice that Kumiko uses various assembly techniques to attach the borders — mitred, or overlapped, or edge to edge.

METRIC CONVERSION

When converting inches to metric equivalents, the amounts have been rounded off to the next highest centimeter when the fraction was .50 or more, and down to the next lowest centimeter when the fraction was .49 or less. For a more precise conversion, use the formula 1 inch = 2.54 cm.

■ Templates for all blocks are provided at the back of the book. Where possible, they are full size. In some cases, pieces are diagrammed on a smaller scale accompanied by the full-size measurements needed. All templates and measurements include a ¼″ (6mm) seam allowance, unless otherwise indicated. Some of the templates need to be reversed for cutting a number of fabric pieces, as indicated on the templates. Take special care in these cases.

■ You will notice that some of the larger template patterns are drawn as if they were folded over, with the topmost portion appearing to be transparent. Templates are often shown this way in Japanese quilting books in order to save space. To make the template, simply make two photocopies of the pattern. Cut out one of each pattern portion along the cutting line and the fold line; flip over the "transparent" portion and tape it to the other portion along the fold line to form the whole template.

■ Instructions are given for making block and quilt tops only. To finish your project, you will need to buy batting and backing fabric, assemble the layers, and quilt them together. Kumiko considers quilting to be an accent, "rather than something to be seen all over the picture." She usually uses silk thread to decorate her quilt tops with *sashiko*-style Japanese embroidery. In quilts used as wall hangings such accent stitching will suffice; however quilts used as bedding will require more extensive quilting. Kumiko seldom draws a design, but usually quilts "freestyle"; in some of the designs in this book, she followed the line of the pattern block, stitching ⅛″ (3mm) away from the seamline. She rarely uses thread to match the fabric — for example, she often uses purple thread for yellow fabric, and green for blue fabric — and may use two or three different thread colors in one quilt.

■ Experiment. Use your imagination. You may want to make a whole quilt or make several individual blocks in different designs. The generous block size makes them ideal for small wall hangings, pillows, or other projects. You can also add to or subtract from the width and number of borders to get a variety of effects and a variety of sizes.

BLOCKS

AND

QUILTS

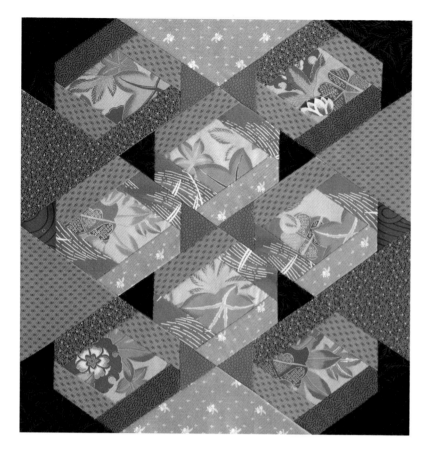

HINAMATSURI

Girls' Festival

On March 3 when the peach trees are in bloom, young girls celebrate Girls' Day and dress in their best kimonos. Each home proudly sets up a beautiful display of court dolls, arranged in five to seven tiers. Emperor, empress, high-ranking premiers, ladies in waiting, and musicians are attired and displayed along with miniature lacquered dishes, bowls, diamond-shaped sweets, and tiny candles with silk shades. Girls invite each other to their homes to taste sweet rice wine and rice crackers and laugh and have fun all day. Every grown-up woman cherishes her memories of the day with nostalgia. I depicted the joyous occasion with floral prints encircled by diamond shapes and red triangle pieces to symbolize a large red spread of the tiers.

INSTRUCTIONS

Cut the required number of fabric pieces as indicated on the templates on page 112. To assemble the block, sew the pieces together in the following sequence, using the diagram as a guide.

1. Sew 2 B pieces to piece A.
2. Sew 2 C pieces to no. 1.
3. Sew 2 D pieces to the ends of no. 2.
4. Repeat steps 1–3 to form 8 diamond units.
5. Sew 2 rows of 3 diamond units each.
6. Sew E, G, and F to the rows and 2 remaining diamond units, according to the diagram.
7. Sew the rows and diamond units together to complete the block.

Block size: 16" × 16" (41cm × 41cm)

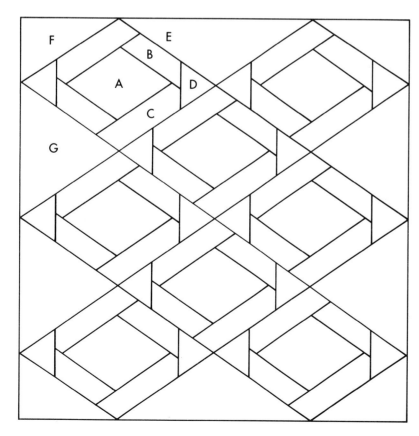

HIKIDASHI

Cardboard Box

I remember playing with little cardboard boxes covered with colorful printed cloth or pretty rice paper. Each had four or five tiny drawers with silk cord handles, and inside each drawer I secretly kept all kinds of memorabilia. They were mostly little trinkets or bric-a-brac and I enjoyed examining every one of them tirelessly after I came home from school. I often wonder where those treasures have gone...and also my youth.

INSTRUCTIONS

Cut the required number of fabric pieces as indicated on the templates on page 113. To assemble the block, sew the pieces together in the following sequence, using the diagram as a guide. This block consists of four identical quarter-blocks turned on end.

1. Sew piece A to piece B.
2. Sew piece C to no. 1.
3. Repeat steps 1 and 2 to make a total of 12 rectangular units.
4. Make 4 quarter-blocks of 3 rectangular units each.
5. Sew the quarter-blocks together, rotating them on end as shown in the diagram to complete the block.

Block size: 16″ × 16″ (41cm × 41cm)

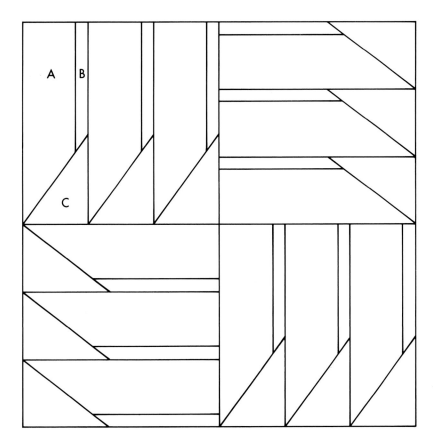

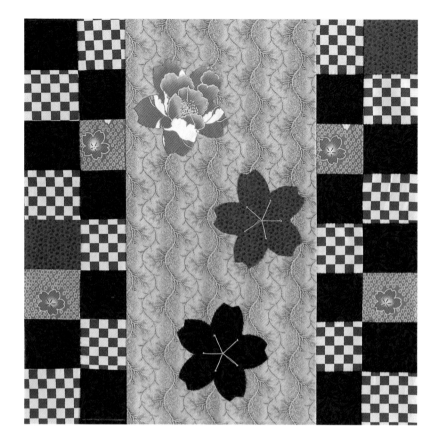

SAKURA

Cherry Blossoms

The cherry blossom is the national flower of Japan. It is often compared to Samurai spirits who linger in this life when needed by the lord, like cherry blossoms which never die on the branches but fall off in the blowing wind. In the early part of April, people have parties under the cherry blossoms, hanging cloth around the trees to make an enclosed area. There they enjoy dancing, singing and lots of food and drink. I depicted the joyous moment by placing checkerboard draperies at both sides with a scattering of cherry blossoms in the center.

INSTRUCTIONS

Cut the required number of fabric pieces as indicated on the templates on page 114. To assemble the block, sew the pieces together in the following sequence, using the diagram as a guide.

1. Sew 4 rows of 8 B pieces each.
2. Sew the rows together in pairs.
3. Appliqué the three A pieces onto piece C.
4. On each flower embroider five French knots with a long stitch from each knot to the center.
5. Sew the rows to the sides of piece C to complete the block.

Block size: 16" × 16" (41cm × 41cm)

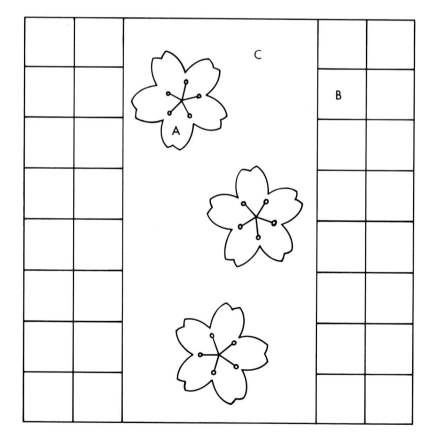

KAMON

Family Crest

家
紋

Family crests were used in the past to distinguish enemy forces from allies on the battlefield, and their use was granted only to nobles and warriors. As years went by, government structure changed. The use of crests gradually spread to ordinary citizens, and today they wear crests with pride in their own family history. In this design I have imitated a family crest and appliquéd it in a butterfly print on a red background as if flower petals are waving. I added a little red triangle at the corner to balance the huge red circle in the center.

CUTTING INSTRUCTIONS

To make one block, cut the required number of pieces indicated on the templates on page 115. To assemble the block, see assembly instructions on page 30. To make a quilt, cut the number of pieces required following the cutting chart.

Block size: 15″ × 15″ (38cm × 38cm)

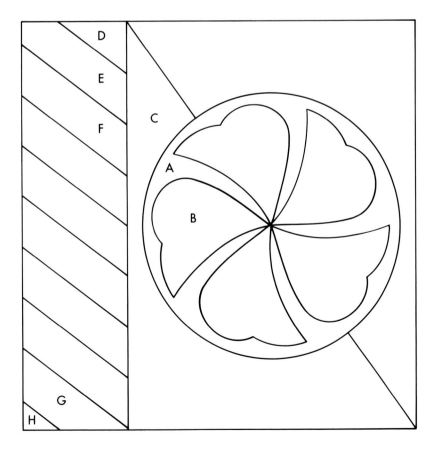

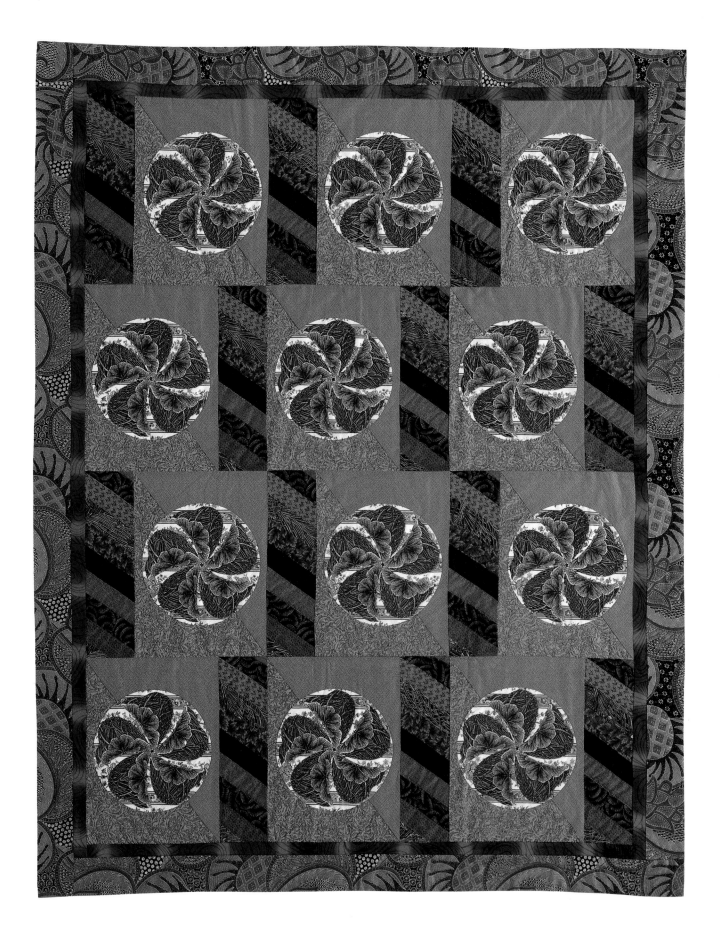

KAMON : *Quilt*

	WALL/CRIB	TWIN	DOUBLE/QUEEN	KING
Size (inches)	53 × 68	68 × 98	83 × 98	98 × 98
Size (centimeters)	135 × 173	173 × 249	211 × 249	249 × 249
Setting	3 × 4	4 × 6	5 × 6	6 × 6
Blocks	12	24	30	36

Fabric needed: *Yards (centimeters) for 45" (114cm) fabric*

	WALL/CRIB	TWIN	DOUBLE/QUEEN	KING
Template A	1 (90)	2 (180)	2½ (220)	2⅞ (260)
Template B	1⅛ (100)	2⅛ (190)	2⅝ (240)	3⅛ (280)
Template C	1⅞ (170)	3¾ (340)	4⅝ (420)	5½ (500)
Template D	¼ (20)	¼ (20)	¼ (20)	⅜ (30)
Template E	⅜ (30)	¾ (60)	⅞ (80)	⅞ (80)
Template F	1 (90)	1¾ (160)	2¼ (200)	2⅝ (240)
Template G	¼ (20)	⅜ (30)	⅜ (30)	½ (40)
Template H	¼ (20)	¼ (20)	¼ (20)	⅜ (30)
Border: 1½" (4cm)	⅜ (30)	½ (40)	½ (40)	⅝ (50)
Border: 3½" (9cm)	2 (180)	2⅞ (260)	2⅞ (260)	2⅞ (260)

Cutting

	WALL/CRIB	TWIN	DOUBLE/QUEEN	KING
Template A	12	24	30	36
Template B	60	120	150	180
Template C	24	48	60	72
Template D	12	24	30	36
Template E	12	24	30	36
Template F	72	144	180	216
Template G	12	24	30	36
Template H	12	24	30	36

Inside border width is 1½" (4cm) including ¼" (6mm) seam allowance.
Outside border width is 3½" (9cm) including ¼" (6mm) seam allowance.

1.

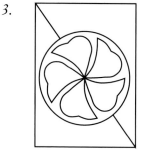

2.

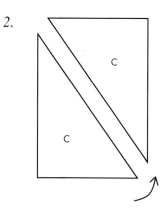

3.

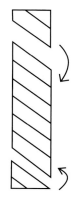

4.

5.

6.

7.

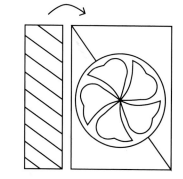

8.

ASSEMBLY INSTRUCTIONS

To assemble each block, sew the pieces together in the following sequence, using the step-by-step drawings and the diagram as a guide.

1. Appliqué all 5 B pieces onto A, forming the crest.
2. Sew together the 2 C pieces, forming a pieced rectangle.
3. Appliqué the crest onto the pieced rectangle.
4. Sew piece D to piece E.
5. Sew the 6 F pieces together, forming a vertical strip.
6. Sew piece G to piece H.
7. Sew no. 4 and no. 6 to no. 5, squaring off the ends.
8. Sew no. 3 to no. 7, completing the block.

If you are making a quilt, assemble and sew together the number of blocks required to complete your project. For example, the quilt shown here is wall hanging size, with twelve blocks sewn in four rows of three blocks each, plus inside and outside borders. Note that the placement of the vertical strips (unit no. 7) alternates from the left to the right side of the block from row to row.

HOKUSAI

北斎

Ukiyo-e Master

Hokusai is known as an Ukiyo-e Master the world over because of his bold composition and color. His favorite subjects were roaring waves of the sea and Mt. Fuji at dawn and sunset. As an homage to the old master I have arranged curved shapes to create a sense of movement and used only his color scheme to symbolize him.

INSTRUCTIONS

Cut the required number of fabric pieces as indicated on the templates on page 117. To assemble the block, sew the pieces together in the following sequence, using the diagram as a guide. The block is made of 9 square units sewn together first in 3 rows.

1. Appliqué C onto D.
2. Appliqué B onto no. 1.
3. Appliqué no. 2 onto A.
4. Repeat steps 1–3 to form a total of 9 square units.
5. Sew the units together in 3 rows.
6. Sew the 3 rows together to complete the block.

Block size: 16″ × 16″ (41cm × 41cm)

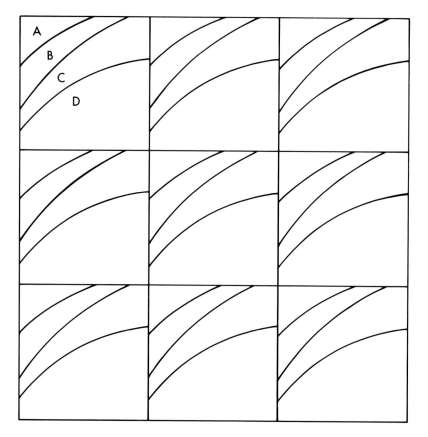

FUNADE

Embarkation

To me, traveling by water is like making a new start in life. The passengers of a cruiseliner are stirred by the blue sky, the blue water, and the sun at its finest.

INSTRUCTIONS

Cut the required number of fabric pieces as indicated on the templates on page 118. To assemble the block, sew the pieces together in the following sequence, using the diagram as a guide.

1. Appliqué the B pieces onto the A pieces to form a total of 4 quarter-circle units.
2. Appliqué the C pieces onto the no. 1 units to form 4 triangular units.
3. Appliqué piece E to the center of piece D.
4. Appliqué the 6 F pieces and the 4 G pieces onto piece D.
5. Sew the corner pieces to D to complete the block.

Block size: 15" × 15" (41cm × 41cm)

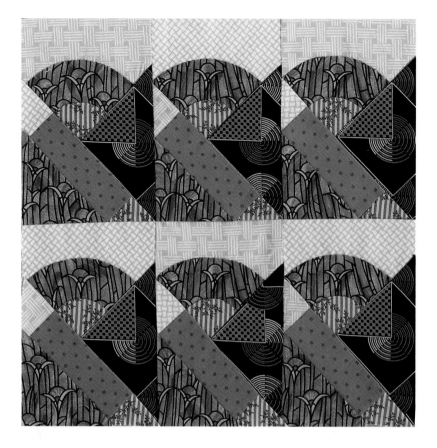

RADIO CITY MUSIC HALL

After an hour-long rehearsal The Rockettes are ready for the real stage. A fanfare breaks the tension and the curtain goes up. Suddenly bright yellowish light illuminates the entire stage while hundreds of star-like tiny blue lights come on looking like inlaid shell. The dancers start kicking their heels high in the air. Outside, many people are already in line in front of Radio City Music Hall for the next performance. Their expectations are high and they hardly notice the cold winter night.

INSTRUCTIONS

Cut the required number of fabric pieces as indicated on the templates on page 120. To assemble the block, sew the pieces together in the following sequence, using the diagram as a guide. This block is made of 6 square units sewn together first in 2 rows.

1. Appliqué piece A to B, and appliqué piece B to C.
2. Sew piece D to no. 1.
3. Sew F and G pieces to piece E.
4. Sew no. 2 to no. 3.
5. Sew piece H to no. 4.
6. Repeat steps 1–5 to make a total of 6 units.
7. Sew the units together in 2 rows of 3 units each.
8. Sew the 2 rows together to complete the block.

Block size: 16" × 16" (41cm × 41cm)

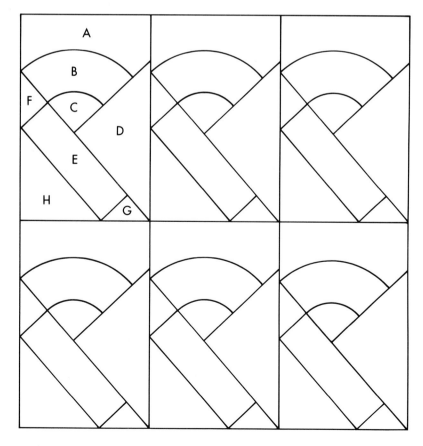

SHOP WINDOWS

Sometimes I get an urge to go out and mingle with the crowd. Between grayish marble structures we find tastefully decorated shop windows. Graceful manikins, fashionably dressed and with blue or green eyes, make us pause. Young girls, pressing their pink cheeks against the glass and nodding to each other, exchange opinions about style. I am on my way home with the only purchase of the day, a box of candy.

INSTRUCTIONS

Cut the required number of fabric pieces as indicated on the templates on page 121. To assemble the block, sew the pieces together in the following sequence, using the diagram as a guide. This block is made of 4 quarter-blocks.

1. Sew the 4 A pieces together in 2 pairs.
2. Sew 2 B pieces to each no. 1 unit.
3. Sew a D piece to a C piece; repeat to form 4 units.
4. Sew 1 no. 3 unit to each no. 2 unit.
5. Sew 1 F piece to each of no. 4 units to form 2 quarter-blocks.
6. Sew the E pieces together in 2 pairs.
7. Sew the 2 remaining no. 3 units to one no. 6, and the 2 remaining F pieces to the other no. 6 to form 2 quarter-blocks.
8. Sew the 4 quarter-blocks together to complete the block.

Block size: 16" × 16" (41cm × 41cm)

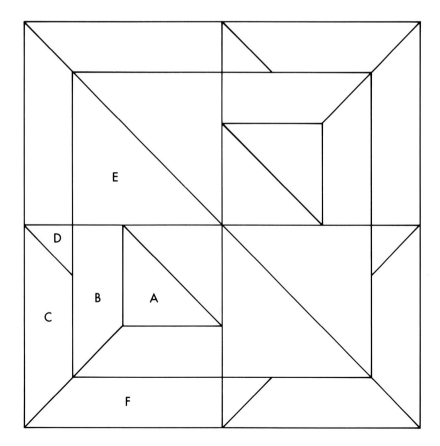

CHO NO MAI 蝶の舞

Dance of the Butterfly

We love a traditional dance called "Dance of the Butterfly." A dancer with a costume covered with a large butterfly design gracefully flitting from one flower to another in springtime is beyond description. I stylized that beautiful feeling with a fan shape of butterfly prints. The square shape represents a dancing stage.

INSTRUCTIONS

Cut the required number of fabric pieces as indicated on the templates on page 123. To assemble the block, sew the pieces together in the following sequence, using the diagram as a guide. This block is made of 9 square units sewn together first in 3 rows.

1. Sew two B pieces together.
2. Sew piece C to no. 1 to form a quarter-circle.
3. Appliqué no. 2 onto piece A to form a square unit.
4. Repeat steps 1–3 to form a total of 9 square units.
5. Sew the square units together in 3 rows of 3 each.
6. Sew the 3 rows together to complete the block.

Block size: 16" × 16" (41cm × 41cm)

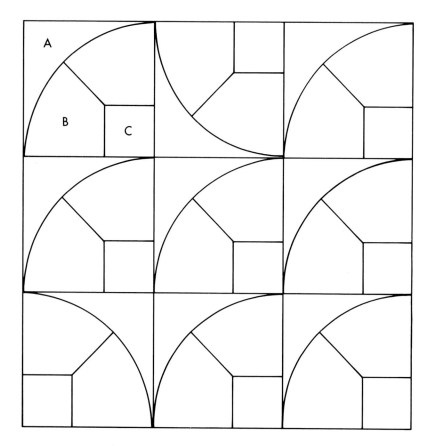

JESTER

A court jester's life revolves around his lord's mood that day. He always must be well prepared to convince his master that he is the funniest man in the court and to keep his master in good humor at all times. To do so he must disguise his true feelings and be pleasant and happy even when he is in the midst of a personal crisis or grief. No matter what, he is constantly busy performing, stumbling on a ball, somersaulting and leaping about.

INSTRUCTIONS

Cut the required number of fabric pieces as indicated on the templates on page 124. To assemble the block, sew the pieces together in the following sequence, using the diagram as a guide. This block is made of 3 rows of 6 units each.

1. Sew piece A to piece B.
2. Appliqué piece C onto no. 1.
3. Appliqué piece D onto no. 2.
4. Repeat steps 1–3 to form a total of 18 rectangular units.
5. Sew the units together in 3 rows of 6 units each.
6. Sew the rows together to complete the block.

Block size: 15 ½" × 15 ½" (39.5cm × 39.5cm)

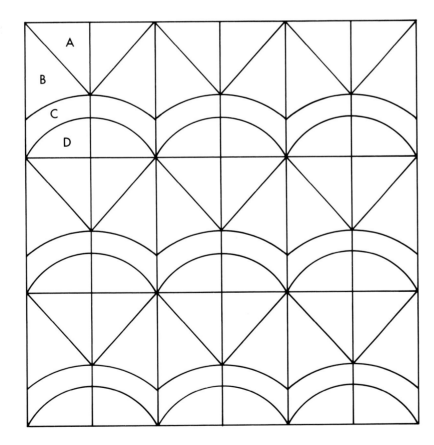

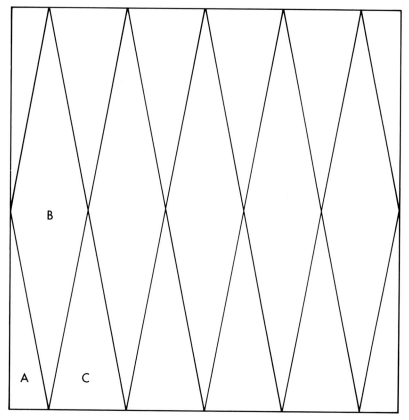

HIZASHI

Sunlight

The rays of the afternoon sun caress the fallen maple leaves in a Japanese garden, taking on reddish autumn tints and creating dark shadows here and there. The remaining chrysanthemums underneath the carpet of leaves linger at season's end.

INSTRUCTIONS

Cut the required number of fabric pieces as indicated on the templates on page 125. To assemble the block, sew the pieces together in the following sequence, using the diagram as a guide. This block is made of diagonal rows with the corner pieces added last.

1. Sew the B and C pieces together in diagonal rows.
2. Sew the rows together.
3. Sew an A piece to each of the 4 corners, completing the block.

Block size: 15" × 15" (38 × 38 cm)

QUATTROCENTO

In the fifteenth century, Italy emerged from the middles ages with an outburst of artistic activity. Today, we witness its sophistication in Italy's splendid quattrocento architecture, paintings and sculptures. It is a breathtaking experience to stroll in the plaza or square in the center of the town, throwing coins in the fountain and feeding birds who peck tidbits from the hand. Ice cream carts entice young and old alike. Tulips in a profusion of colors are so pleasant to the eyes that time briefly ceases to exist.

CUTTING INSTRUCTIONS

To make one block, cut the required number of pieces indicated on the templates on page 126. To assemble the block, see assembly instructions on page 42. To make a quilt, cut the number of pieces required following the cutting chart.

Block Size: 15" × 15" (38cm × 38cm)

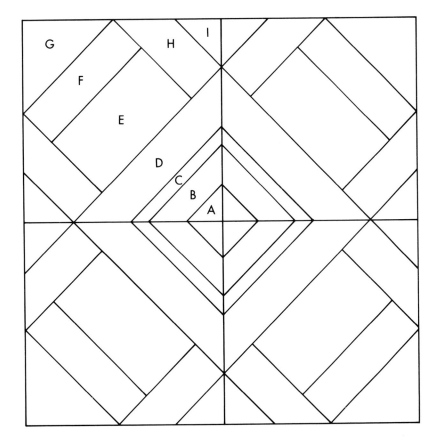

QUATTROCENTO : *Quilt*

	WALL/CRIB	TWIN	DOUBLE/QUEEN	KING
Size (inches)	47 × 47	77 × 92	92 × 92	107 × 107
Size (centimeters)	119 × 119	196 × 234	234 × 234	272 × 272
Setting	3 × 3	5 × 6	6 × 6	7 × 7
Blocks	9	30	36	49

Fabric needed: *Yards (centimeters) for 45" (114cm) fabric*

Template A	¼ (20)	½ (40)	⅝ (50)	¾ (60)
Template B	⅜ (30)	⅞ (80)	⅞ (80)	1¼ (110)
Template C	⅜ (30)	⅞ (80)	⅞ (80)	1⅛ (100)
Template D	¾ (60)	2 (180)	2⅛ (190)	2⅞ (260)
Template E	¾ (60)	2 (180)	2⅛ (190)	2⅞ (260)
Template F	½ (40)	1⅛ (100)	1¼ (110)	1⅝ (150)
Template G	⅜ (30)	1 (90)	1⅛ (100)	1½ (130)
Template H	¾ (60)	2 (180)	2⅜ (210)	3¼ (290)
Template I	⅜ (30)	⅞ (80)	1 (90)	1⅜ (120)
Border: 1½" (4cm)	⅜ (30)	½ (40)	½ (40)	⅝ (50)

Cutting

Template A	36	120	144	196
Template B	36	120	144	196
Template C	36	120	144	196
Template D	36	120	144	196
Template E	36	120	144	196
Template F	36	120	144	196
Template G	36	120	144	196
Template H	72	240	288	392
Template I	72	240	288	392

Border width is 1½" (4cm) including ¼" (6mm) seam allowance.

1.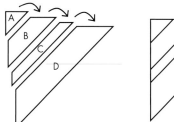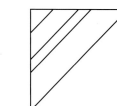

 2.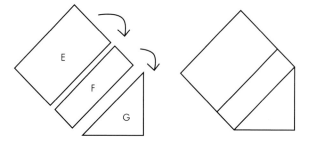

3.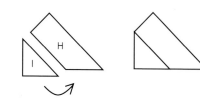

4.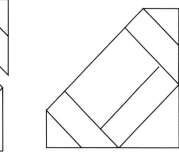

5.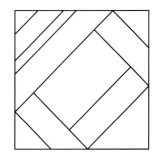

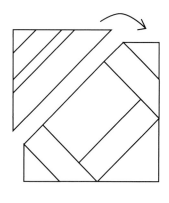

ASSEMBLY INSTRUCTIONS

To assemble each block, sew the pieces together in the following sequence, using the step-by-step drawings and the diagram as a guide.

1. Sew A, B, C, and D together; repeat to form a total of 4 triangular units.
2. Sew E, F, and G together; repeat to form a total of 4 pieced units.
3. Sew H and I together; repeat to form a total of 8 pieced units.
4. Sew 2 no. 3 units to each no. 2 unit.
5. Sew a no. 1 unit to each no. 4 unit; repeat to form 4 quarter-blocks.
6. Sew the 4 quarter-blocks together to complete the block.

6.

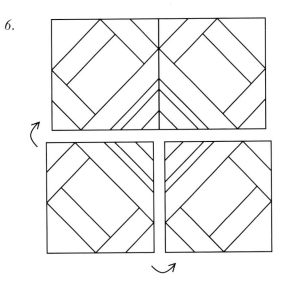

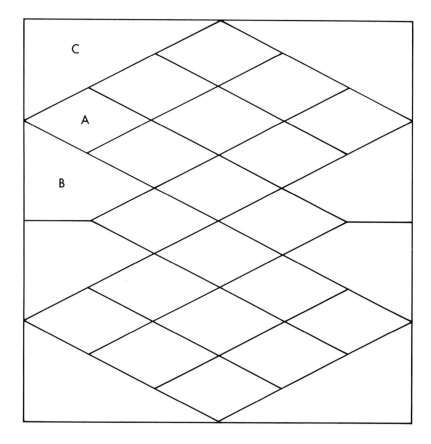

MATSUKASA

Pinecones

Like the redheaded crane, pine trees are beloved among Japanese. Because of their strength and longevity, they are often used in kimono designs, paintings, and interior decorations. Here I have illustrated a pile of pine cones in an abstract manner, gradually changing their colors from green to brown on the bark-littered background.

INSTRUCTIONS

Cut the required number of fabric pieces as indicated on the templates on page 127. To assemble the block, sew the pieces together in the following sequence, using the diagram as a guide. The A pieces are first sewn together in diagonal rows, with the side and corner pieces added last.

1. Sew 4 rows of 3 A pieces each.
2. Sew 2 rows of 4 A pieces each.
3. Sew the A rows together following the diagram.
4. Sew the B pieces to no. 3; sew adjacent B seams together.
5. Sew the C pieces to the corners to complete the block.

Block size: 16" × 16" (41cm × 41cm)

KANZASHI

Girl's Hair Decoration

In Japan, young girls celebrate New Year's day by wearing a kimono and an old fashioned hairdo. They decorate their hair with many beautiful accessories such as silk flowers that dangle on the forehead, silk bands in orange and light blue tie-dyes, lacquered combs, and tortoiseshell pins. All of these orchestrate the black hairdo and enhance the young girls' blushing cheeks.

INSTRUCTIONS

Cut the required number of fabric pieces as indicated on the templates on page 128. To assemble the block, sew the pieces together in the following sequence, using the diagram as a guide. This block is made of 4 rows sewn together.

1. Sew piece A to piece B.
2. Sew piece C to no. 1
3. Sew piece D to no. 2.
4. Repeat steps 1–3 to form a total of 8 units.
5. Sew the units to the remaining D pieces, making 4 rows.
6. Sew the rows together, completing the block.

Block size: 16" × 16" (41cm × 41cm)

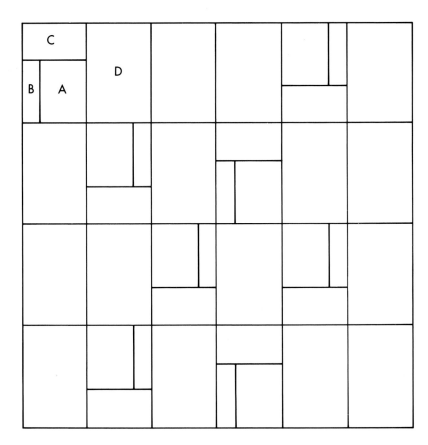

DOWNTOWN

Christmas is just around the corner. It has snowed overnight, making the tiny colored lights that decorate the trees glow more brightly, exciting shoppers as they cross the busy intersection. Snow has started falling again and the shop windows reflect the displays inside like a rainbow. Everywhere children's hearts are pounding with great expectations.

INSTRUCTIONS

Cut the required number of fabric pieces as indicated on the templates on page 129. To assemble the block, sew the pieces together in the following sequence, using the diagram as a guide. This block is made of 3 rows of 3 units each.

1. Sew 4 B pieces to each A piece, forming 4 square units.
2. Sew 2 B pieces to each C piece, forming 2 triangular units.
3. Sew one D piece to each no. 2 unit, forming 2 square units.
4. Sew the remaining D pieces together in pairs, forming 3 square units.
5. Sew units no. 1, no. 3 and no. 4 together, as pictured, first in 3 rows of three; then sew the rows together to complete the block.

Block size: 15 ¾" × 15 ¾" (40cm × 40cm)

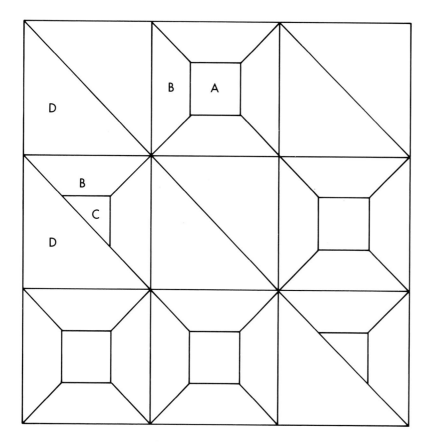

FUYUDORI

Migratory Birds

On winter days you can see redheaded cranes shivering in the extreme northern regions of Japan. They are treated as the symbols of Japan because people believe in the birds' longevity and because the red head transmits a sense of the rising sun to the Japanese people. This is the reason the cranes are the most sought out design in dishes, interior decorations, and kimonos, especially on happy occasions like weddings, birthdays, and New Year's Day. Here I have simplified all those occasions in a small block depicting cranes flying over wintry water and frosted plains.

INSTRUCTIONS

Cut the required number of fabric pieces as indicated on the templates on page 130. To assemble the block, sew the pieces together in the following sequence, using the diagram as a guide. This block is made of 4 rows sewn together.

1. Sew the A pieces together in 2 rows of 8 each.
2. Sew the B pieces together in 2 rows of 10 each.
3. Sew rows no. 1 and no. 2 together, following the diagram, to complete the block.

Block size: 16" × 16" (41cm × 41cm)

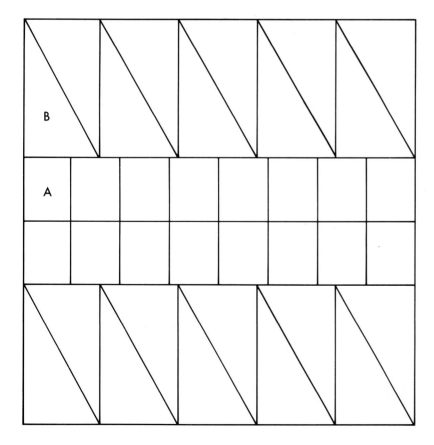

MORNING GLORY

Sunbathers on the beach are enjoying the afternoon sun. Colorful parasols are every-where; with their patterns of stripes and checks they look like blooming morning glo-ries in the sea breeze. Children are chasing each other with glee, disturbing the sun bathers as they try to nap. A long green hill covered with evening primroses along the dunes presents a breathtaking view.

INSTRUCTIONS

Cut the required number of fabric pieces as indicated on the templates on page 130. To assemble the block, sew the pieces together in the following sequence, using the diagram as a guide. This block is made of 4 quarter-blocks.

1. Sew A - B - C - B - C - B - A in order, to make a half-circle.
2. Sew 2 D pieces together.
3. Appliqué no. 1 onto no. 2.
4. Sew 2 E pieces together.
5. Sew no. 4 to piece F.
6. Sew no. 5 to piece G.
7. Sew no. 6 to piece H.
8. Sew no. 7 to piece I.
9. Sew no. 8 to no. 3, to form a quarter-block.
10. Repeat steps 1–9 to make a total of 4 quarter-blocks; then sew the quarter-blocks together to complete the block.

Block size: 16" × 16" (41cm × 41cm)

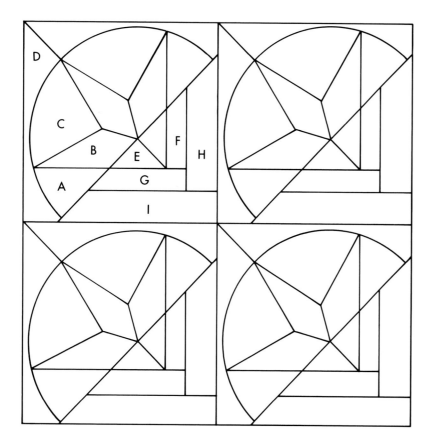

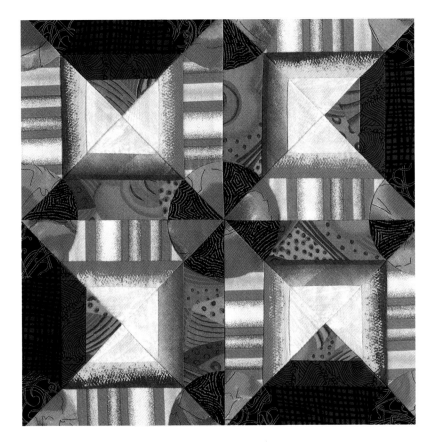

OPERA HOUSE

The final act is taking place. In a gorgeous eighteenth-century royal court scene, the primadonna is about to die in the arms of the tenor. As the duet reaches its climax, the audience has tears in their eyes. In the cold winter night, under the gaslight, by the horse carriages, the chauffeurs patiently await their masters.

INSTRUCTIONS

Cut the required number of fabric pieces as indicated on the templates on page 132. To assemble the block, sew the pieces together in the following sequence, using the diagram as a guide.

1. Sew 1 A piece to each B piece, forming 16 small triangle units.
2. Appliqué two D pieces to each C piece.
3. Sew each no. 1 triangle to a no. 2, forming 16 larger triangular units.
4. Sew 4 no. 3 triangular units together, forming 4 quarter-blocks.
5. Sew the quarter-blocks together, completing the block.

Block size: 16" × 16" (41cm × 41cm)

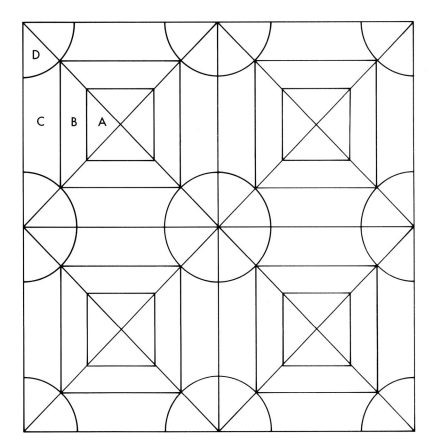

EGYPTIAN FAN

During the Art Deco period, Egyptian designs were very much in fashion and used in interior decoration. Imagine women of high society lounging with beautifully designed Egyptian fans in their hands, enjoying sweet cocktails, playing cards, and gossiping. The high walls surrounding them are made of blue marble to cool the room.

INSTRUCTIONS

Cut the required number of fabric pieces as indicated on the templates on page 133. To assemble the block, sew the pieces together in the following sequence, using the diagram as a guide. This block is made of 4 quarter-blocks with the border attached last.

1. Appliqué the B, C, and D pieces onto the A pieces, to form 4 center units.
2. Sew the 4 no. 1 units together.
3. Sew the E pieces onto the sides of no. 2.
4. Sew the F pieces onto the corners of no. 3, completing the block.

Block size: 16" × 16" (41cm × 41cm)

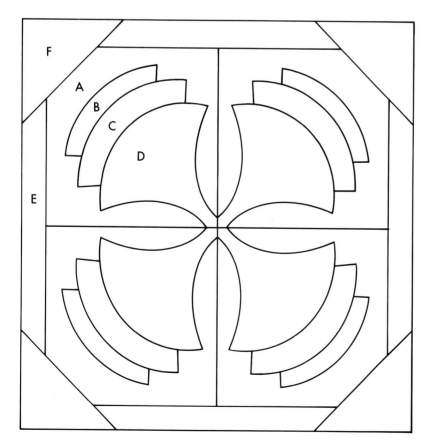

TOPKAPI

Istanbul, the ancient capital of the Ottoman Dynasty of the Turkish Empire sits astride two worlds: Byzantine and Ottoman. It is the most beautiful skyline that undulates between heaven and earth, and Topkapi Palace is home to dazzling, priceless jewels that once decorated kings and queens. On the magnificent mosaic floor of the palace a unique medallion carpet displays the beauty of its design and technique.

CUTTING INSTRUCTIONS

To make one block, cut the required number of pieces indicated on the templates on page 135. To assemble the block, see assembly instructions on page 54. To make a quilt, cut the number of pieces required following the cutting chart.

Block Size: 16" × 16" (41cm × 41cm)

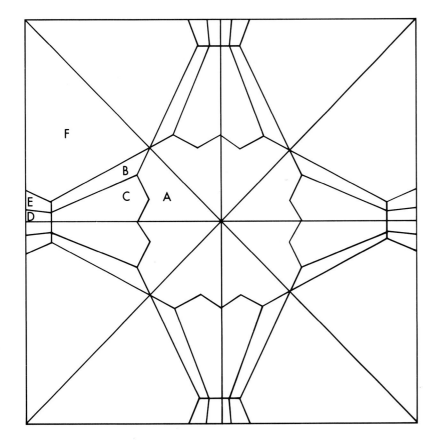

TOPKAPI : *Quilt*

	WALL/CRIB	TWIN	DOUBLE/QUEEN	KING
Size (inches)	54 × 70	70 × 86	86 × 86	102 × 102
Size (centimeters)	137 × 178	178 × 218	218 × 218	259 × 259
Setting	3 × 4	4 × 5	5 × 5	6 × 6
Blocks	12	20	25	36

Fabric needed: Yards (centimeters) for 45" (114cm) fabric

Template A	1¼ (100)	1¾ (160)	2½ (220)	3⅛ (280)
Template B	½ (40)	¾ (60)	⅞ (80)	1⅛ (100)
Template C	1¼ (100)	1¾ (160)	2¼ (200)	3⅛ (280)
Template D	½ (40)	¾ (60)	⅞ (80)	1⅛ (100)
Template E	⅜ (30)	⅝ (50)	¾ (60)	⅞ (80)
Template F	2¾ (250)	4⅝ (420)	5¾ (520)	8 (740)
Border: 1½" (4cm)	⅜ (30)	⅜ (30)	½ (40)	⅝ (50)
Border: 2½" (6cm)	2⅛ (190)	2½ (230)	2½ (230)	3 (270)

Cutting

Template A	96	160	200	288
Template B	96	160	200	288
Template C	96	160	200	288
Template D	96	160	200	288
Template E	96	160	200	288
Template F	96	160	200	288

Inside border width is 1½" (4cm) including ¼" (6mm) seam allowance.
Outside border width is 2½" (6cm) including ¼" (6mm) seam allowance.

1.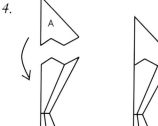

2.

3.

4.

5.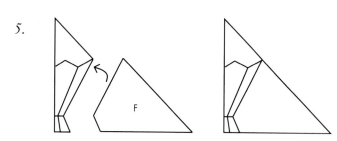

6.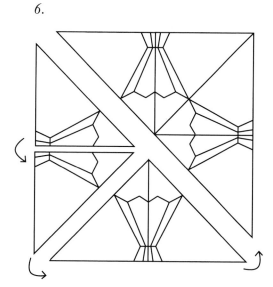

To assemble each block, sew the pieces together in the following sequence, using the step-by-step drawings and the piecing diagram as a guide.

1. Sew 1 B piece to 1 C piece.
2. Sew 1 D piece to 1 E piece.
3. Sew no. 1 to no. 2.
4. Appliqué 1 A piece onto no. 3.
5. Sew 1 F piece to no. 4 to make a triangular unit.
6. Repeat steps 1–5 to make a total of 8 triangular units; sew the 8 units together to complete the block.

If you are making a quilt, assemble and sew together the number of blocks required to complete your project. For example, the quilt shown here is wall hanging size, with twelve blocks sewn in four rows of three blocks each, plus an inside and outside border.

PLANETARIUM

The planetarium is one of the school children's favorite places. Under the teacher's watchful eye, they sit quietly in their seats. The dark sky with its twinkling stars expands overhead and everyone is bathed in its mysterious atmosphere. After observing the various constellations, the galaxy, and the movements of heavenly bodies, we leave this dream world and enter the bold daylight filled with noisy automobiles, barking dogs, and people passing swiftly by.

INSTRUCTIONS

Cut the required number of fabric pieces as indicated on the templates on page 136. To assemble the block, sew the pieces together in the following sequence, using the diagram as a guide. This block is made of 4 quarter-blocks.

1. Appliqué 1 A piece onto each B piece, forming 16 small quarter-circles.
2. Appliqué 1 C piece onto each D piece.
3. Appliqué 1 no. 1 onto each no. 2, forming 16 square units.
4. Sew 4 no. 3 square units together, forming 4 quarter-blocks.
5. Sew the quarter-blocks together to complete the block.

Block size: 16" × 16" (41cm × 41cm)

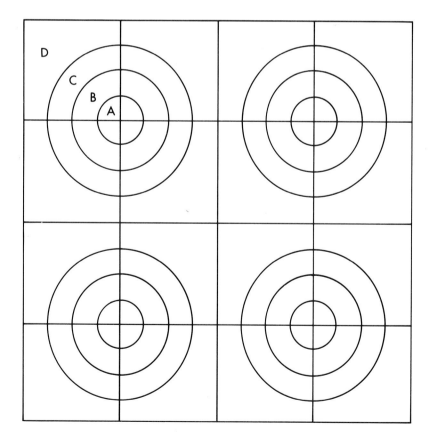

ANTIQUE RADIO

Once it was a luxury to own a radio at home. My father was the first to own one in the small town where we lived, and all the neighborhood kids swarmed around the radio with much curiosity and noisy comments. They were all amazed by the sound of the radio and its fancy facade of decorative fabric. Today kids are crazy about Teenage Mutant Ninja Turtle videos.

INSTRUCTIONS

Cut the required number of fabric pieces as indicated on the templates on page 137. To assemble the block, sew the pieces together in the following sequence, using the diagram as a guide. This block is made of 4 quarter-blocks.

1. Appliqué 2 B pieces onto each A piece.
2. Appliqué 2 C pieces onto each no. 1.
3. Sew 2 D pieces to each no. 2, forming 4 quarter-blocks.
4. Sew the quarter-blocks together to complete the block.

Block size: 16″ × 16″ (41cm × 41cm)

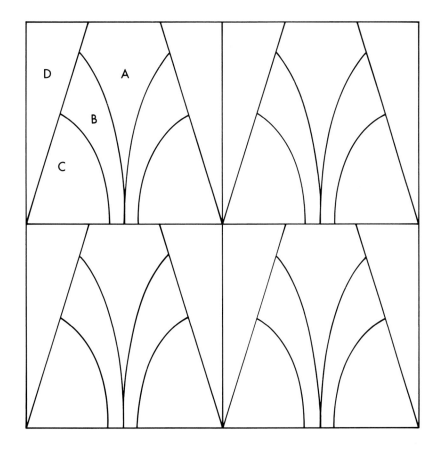

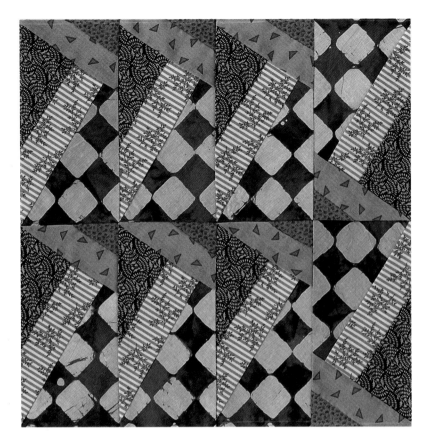

INDY 500

The fiercely competing race cars are on the last stretch. The winner's flag flashes downward with a swishing sound in the crisp air. The cries of spectators and roaring engines stir the atmosphere, and the crowd sways like huge waves in the distance.

INSTRUCTIONS

Cut the required number of fabric pieces as indicated on the templates on page 138. To assemble the block, sew the pieces together in the following sequence, using the diagram as a guide.

1. Sew piece A to piece B.
2. Sew piece C to D and D to E.
3. Sew no. 1 and no. 2 together.
4. Repeat steps 1–3 to form a total of 8 rectangular units.
5. Sew the units together in 2 rows of 4 each.
6. Sew the rows together to complete the block.

Block size: 16″ × 16″ (41cm × 41cm)

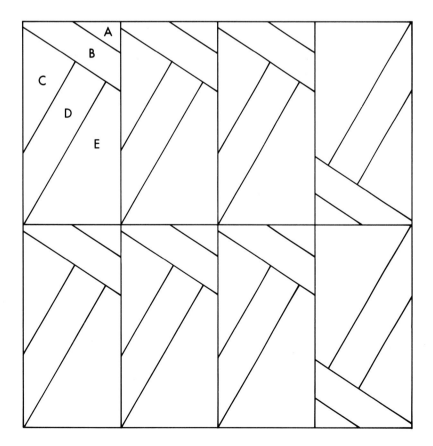

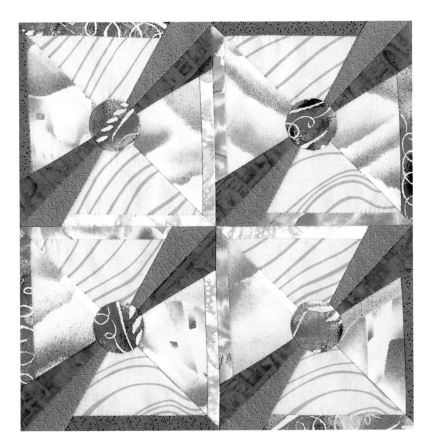

PROPELLERS

In the vast blue sky of a summer day you will find many propellers flying in a circular motion or performing loop-the-loops. Some are flying in formation, marked by white contrails. They keep soaring all day until they notice that the blue sky is being bathed red by the sunset.

INSTRUCTIONS

Cut the required number of fabric pieces as indicated on the templates on page 139. To assemble the block, sew the pieces together in the following sequence, using the diagram as a guide. This block is made of 4 quarter-blocks sewn together.

1. Sew two A pieces together; repeat to make a second unit.
2. Sew two B pieces to each no. 1 unit.
3. Sew 2 C pieces to each no. 1.
4. Sew the 2 no. 3 units together.
5. Appliqué D onto no. 4.
6. Repeat steps 1–5 to form a total of 4 quarter-blocks.
7. Sew the quarter-blocks together, following the diagram, to complete the block.

Block size: 16″ × 16″ (41cm × 41cm)

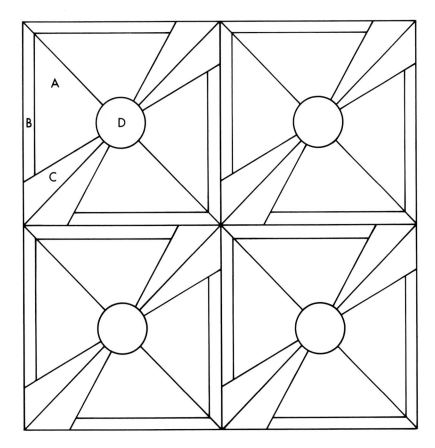

IRORI

Hearth

When I was a child, I visited my grand-mother's home in the northern countryside. The farmhouse had a square-shaped hearth in the center of the living room. A kettle on a swirl-shaped trivet would be intermit-tently whistling and wood would be constantly burning to keep warm the family chatting around it.

INSTRUCTIONS

Cut the required number of fabric pieces as indicated on the templates on page 140. To assemble the block, sew the pieces together in the following sequence, using the diagram as a guide.

1. Sew piece A to piece B.
2. Sew four C pieces to no. 1, overlapping as necessary.
3. Sew four D pieces to no. 2.
4. Repeat steps 1, 2, and 3 to form a total of 9 square units.
5. Sew one F piece to each of 5 E pieces to form 5 strips.
6. Sew the 2 G pieces to the ends of the remaining E piece to form 1 strip.
7. Sew the strips and squares together, follow-ing the diagram.

Block size: 16" × 16" (41cm × 41cm)

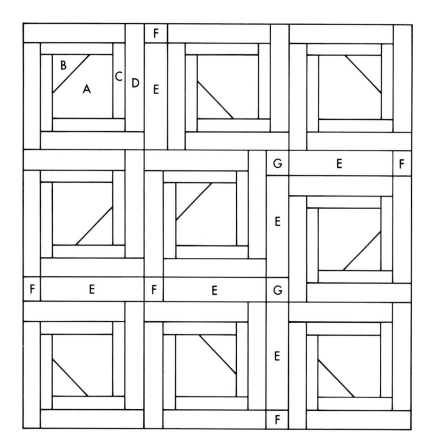

MATSURI

Folk Festival

There are many festivals throughout the year in all regions of Japan, and they often include bonfires dedicated to Buddha and God. High mountains are regarded as places where gods reside. Here I depicted red mountains blushed by vigorously burning fires that contrast with dark silent mountains and present a mysterious atmosphere.

INSTRUCTIONS

Cut the required number of fabric pieces as indicated on the templates on page 140. To assemble the block, sew the pieces together in the following sequence, using the diagram as a guide. This block is made of 9 square units sewn together first in 3 rows.

1. Sew A, B, and C together.
2. Sew D, E, and F together.
3. Sew no. 1, no. 2, and G together.
4. Repeat steps 1–3 to form a total of 4 corner units.
5. Repeat steps 1, 2, and 1; sew together to form the center unit.
6. Sew H and I together.
7. Sew 2 J pieces and K together.
8. Sew no. 6 and no. 7 together.
9. Repeat steps 6, 7, and 8 to form the 4 remaining units.
10. Sew the units together in strips of 3.
11. Sew the 3 strips together to form the block.

Block size: 16″ × 16″ (41cm × 41cm)

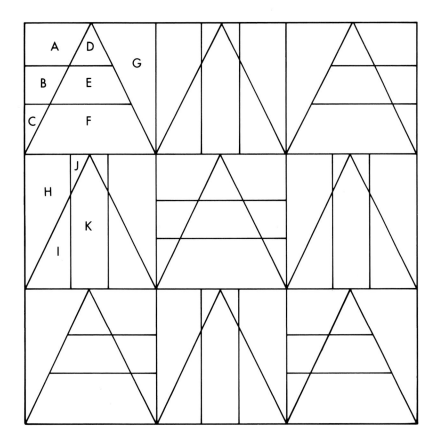

CLEOPATRA

Many servants stand in their thin clothing with peacock-feather fans in hand, while two attendants at the entrance grip sunshades with long fringes. They are all awaiting the queen of Egypt's appearance on the balcony. The green water gently flows by, carrying floating lotus flowers in the full flower of their bloom; the cattails proudly hold their upright postures. In the queen's glittering room there are many valuable treasures, including Caesar's crown.

INSTRUCTIONS

Cut the required number of fabric pieces as indicated on the templates on page 142. To assemble the block, sew the pieces together in the following sequence, using the diagram as a guide.

1. Appliqué 1 B piece onto each C piece to form 4 wedge-shaped units.
2. Sew 1 no. 1 to each of the 4 D pieces to form 4 larger wedges.
3. Sew the 4 no. 2 wedge shapes together to form a circle.
4. Appliqué piece A onto no. 3.
5. Appliqué the 4 E pieces onto the 4 F pieces.
6. Sew the no. 5 units to the no. 3 circle unit.
7. Appliqué one G piece onto each side of an H piece; repeat to form 4 fan shapes.
8. Appliqué the no. 7 units onto no. 6, forming the center unit.
9. Sew the I pieces onto the corners to complete the block.

Block size: 16" × 16" (41cm × 41cm)

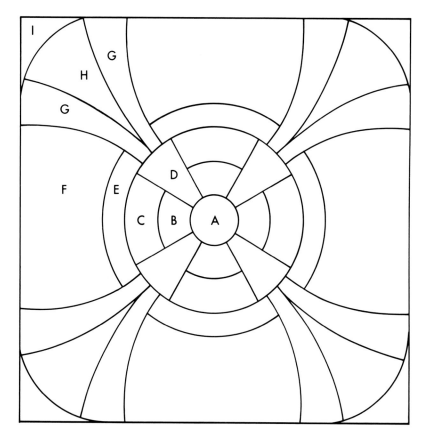

TROPICAL GARDEN

In the glass house, exotic flowers are in full bloom and give off their fragrance in abundance. Many rare birds are happy in the environment and flit from one flower to another, feasting on the sweet nectar. This design depicts an earthly paradise with all the necessary elements in one big flower at the center.

CUTTING INSTRUCTIONS

To make one block, cut the required number of pieces indicated on the templates on page 144. To assemble the block, see assembly instructions on page 66. To make a quilt, cut the number of pieces required following the cutting chart.

Block Size: 16" × 16" (41cm × 41cm)

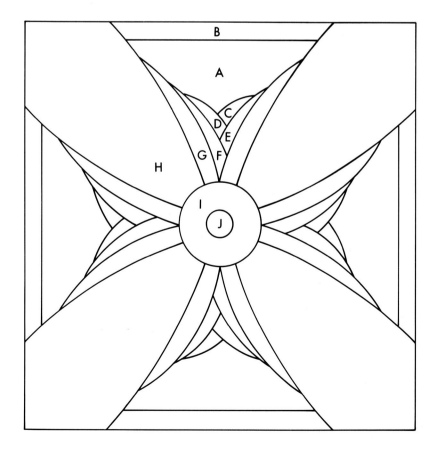

TROPICAL GARDEN : *Quilt*

	WALL/CRIB	TWIN	DOUBLE/QUEEN	KING
Size (inches)	50 × 66	66 × 98	82 × 98	114 × 114
Size (centimeters)	127 × 168	168 × 249	208 × 249	290 × 290
Setting	3 × 4	4 × 6	5 × 6	7 × 7
Blocks	12	24	30	49

Fabric needed: *Yards (centimeters) for 45" (114cm) fabric*

Template A	⅞ (80)	1½ (130)	1¾ (160)	2⅞ (260)
Template B	⅞ (80)	1½ (130)	1¾ (160)	2⅞ (260)
Template C	¼ (20)	⅜ (30)	½ (40)	¾ (60)
Template D	⅜ (30)	½ (40)	⅝ (50)	⅞ (80)
Template E	⅜ (30)	⅝ (50)	¾ (60)	1⅛ (100)
Template F	½ (40)	⅞ (80)	1 (90)	1½ (130)
Template G	⅞ (80)	1¾ (160)	2⅛ (190)	3⅜ (310)
Template H	2 (180)	3⅞ (350)	4¾ (430)	7½ (690)
Template I	⅜ (30)	½ (40)	⅝ (50)	⅞ (80)
Template J	¼ (20)	¼ (20)	¼ (20)	¼ (20)
Border: 1½" (4cm)	⅜ (30)	½ (40)	½ (40)	⅝ (50)

Cutting

Template A	48	96	120	196
Template B	48	96	120	196
Template C	48	96	120	196
Template D	48	96	120	196
Template E	48	96	120	196
Template F	48	96	120	196
Template G	96	192	240	392

	WALL/CRIB	TWIN	DOUBLE/QUEEN	KING
Template H	12	24	30	49
Template I	12	24	30	49
Template J	12	24	30	49

Border width is 1½" (4cm) including ¼" (6mm) seam allowance.

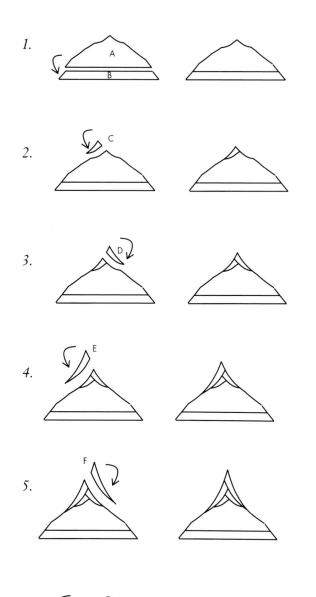

1.

2.

3.

4.

5.

6.

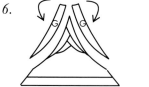
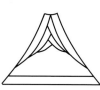
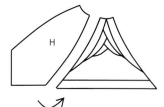
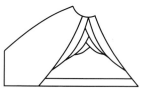

ASSEMBLY INSTRUCTIONS

To assemble each block, sew the pieces together in the following sequence, using the step-by-step drawings and the diagram as a guide.

1. Sew piece A to piece B.
2. Appliqué piece C onto no. 1.
3. Appliqué piece D onto no. 2.
4. Appliqué piece E onto no. 3.
5. Appliqué piece F onto no. 4.
6. Appliqué 2 G pieces onto no. 5.
7. Appliqué H onto no. 6.
8. Repeat steps 1–7, making a total of 4 pieced units.
9. Appliqué the 4 pieced units to each other, forming a square unit.
10. Appliqué piece J onto piece I, forming the center piece, and appliqué the center piece onto the square unit to complete the block.

If you are making a quilt, assemble and sew together the number of blocks required to complete your project. For example, the quilt shown here is wall hanging size, with twelve blocks sewn in 3 rows of 4 blocks each, plus a border.

8. & 9.

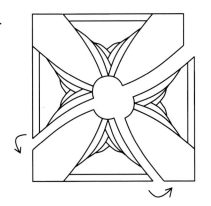

10.

SAFARI

Broad sky, strong wind, huge sun, vast earth, roaming lions, the heartbeat sound of drums; these are my conceptions of Africa. The burning sun is about to hide below the horizon and darkness starts to wrap the entire hemisphere. And I see twinkling yellow spots here and there, a hissing sound, noise of animals, and singing nightingales. I retreat to the camp fire but I can hardly go back to sleep with such a thundering in my heart.

INSTRUCTIONS

Cut the required number of fabric pieces as indicated on the templates on page 146. To assemble the block, sew the pieces together in the following sequence, using the diagram as a guide.

1. Appliqué B, C, and D in order onto A.
2. Sew no. 1 to the 4 F pieces.
3. Appliqué J onto I to make a total of 4 corner units.
4. Appliqué 2 E pieces and 2 no. 3 units onto no. 2.
5. Sew 2 H pieces to each G, to make a total of 4 units.
6. Sew no. 4 and no. 5 together.
7. Appliqué the 2 remaining no. 3 units and 2 E pieces to no. 6 to complete the block.

Block size: 16" × 16" (41cm × 41cm)

MIRROR BALL

The dance hall is packed with men and women dancing. Polka dots, paisley bow ties, and sheer silk chiffon dresses with dangling fringes reflect off the mirror ball on the ceiling. Colorful lights shooting from backstage change the shade of the mirror ball from moment to moment and excite romping dancers. The night air is still young.

INSTRUCTIONS

Cut the required number of fabric pieces as indicated on the templates on page 149. To assemble the block, sew the pieces together in the following sequence, using the diagram as a guide.

1. Appliqué C onto B, and then B onto A, forming the center unit.
2. Appliqué E onto D, then F onto E, and G onto F.
3. Repeat step 2 to form a total of 4 pieced units.
4. Appliqué the no. 3 units to each other, overlapping the G edges onto the D edges.
5. Appliqué the center unit to no. 4 to complete the block.

Block size: 16″ × 16″ (41cm × 41cm)

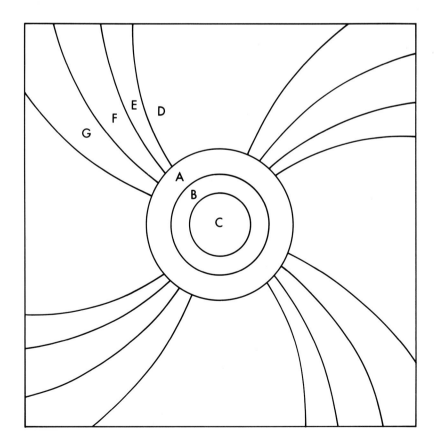

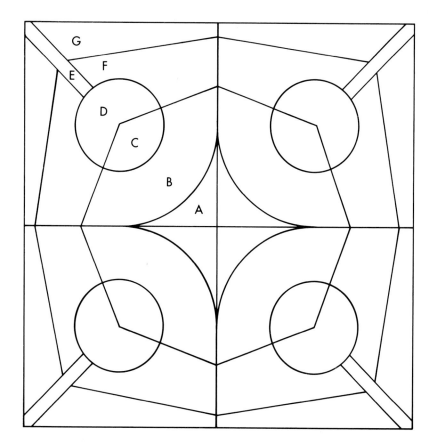

UCHIWA TO SENSU

Japanese Fans

I combined two types of fans in this block. One, called "Uchiwa," is used more often as a kitchen gadget than for cooling oneself. The other type is called "Sensu" and has a more fashionable use; it is an important accessory when formally dressed in a kimono. Sensu is also used as a device to express the feelings of performers on stage such as Kabuki and "Noh" play. This fan is also used by dancers and storytellers as stage props. Both fans are necessities in Japanese daily life even in today's computer age.

INSTRUCTIONS

Cut the required number of fabric pieces as indicated on the templates on page 152. To assemble the block, sew the pieces together in the following sequence, using the diagram as a guide. This block is made of 4 quarter-blocks.

1. Appliqué B onto A and C onto B.
2. Sew F and G together; repeat to form another F–G unit.
3. Appliqué E to one no. 2, and then to the other no. 2.
4. Appliqué D onto no. 3.
5. Appliqué no. 1 to no. 4.
6. Repeat steps 1–5 to form a total of 4 quarter-blocks.
7. Sew the 4 quarter-blocks together to make the complete block.

Block size: 16" × 16" (41cm × 41cm)

KASUMI

A Hazy Sky

When I lived in Kamakura, I sometimes saw a most unusual morning sky. It reminded me of the classical prints I saw in school, and I thought about how many years ago Japanese probably enjoyed seeing the same beautiful sky. The greenish shapes on the top and bottom of this design are traditional Japanese motifs called Kasumi, which are used in classic paintings and kimono designs to symbolize a hazy sky or mist. The many-patterned clouds reflect the morning sunlight and contrast against the dark background. The scattered circular bluish prints suggest fog in the morning.

INSTRUCTIONS

Cut the required number of fabric pieces as indicated on the templates on page 154. All templates include a ¼″ (6mm) seam allowance, except for L and M, which require that you add a ⅛″ (6mm) seam allowance because the shapes have such tight curves.

Following the diagram, place, pin, and appliqué all pieces onto the 16″×16″ square background piece (N), in the following order: A, D, all F pieces, G, H, I, J, K, B, C, E, L, and M.

Block size: 16″×16″ (41cm×41cm)

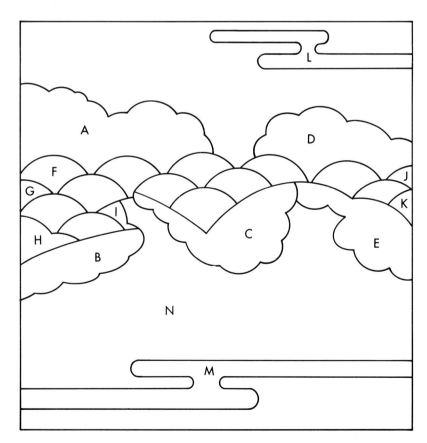

PHONOGRAPH

I can still remember playing a record on the phonograph. It required constant cranking of the handle, and sometimes I needed to put a new stylus in the sound arm. I also had to be alert to catch the moment the record ended its music; otherwise, I was bothered by the scratching noise. Today we enjoy more sophisticated sound systems and we do not remember what happened to the old phonograph, yet I miss the squeaky sound of the old gramophone with its high-pitched voices.

INSTRUCTIONS

Cut the required number of fabric pieces as indicated on the templates on page 157. To assemble the block, sew the pieces together in the following sequence, using the diagram as a guide.

1. Sew 2 B pieces together; repeat to form a total of 4 quarter-circles.
2. Appliqué each no. 1 onto 1 A to form 4 squares.
3. Sew the 4 squares together to form the center unit.
4. Sew the C pieces together in 2 pairs.
5. Sew the F pieces together in pairs.
6. Appliqué 1 D piece onto each no. 4 unit.
7. Appliqué 1 D piece onto each no. 5 unit.
8. Sew the no. 7 units to the top and bottom of the center unit.
9. Sew an E piece to each end of the no. 6 units.
10. Sew the no. 9 units to the sides of the center unit to complete the block.

Block size: 16"×16" (41cm×41cm)

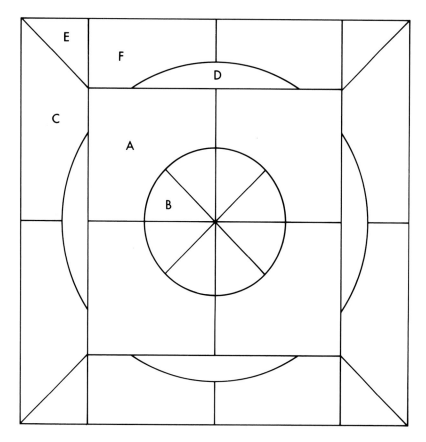

SPACE CENTER

At the space center in America, many elite scientists work long hours. This world-renowned space laboratory is a most glorious facility that has propelled many astronauts into space. In this design, I was thinking about the most advanced rocket being readied for firing and the celebrated technicians who are busy examining every detail of the complicated components and operational sequences.

CUTTING INSTRUCTIONS

To make one block, cut the required number of pieces indicated on the templates on page 159. To assemble the block, see assembly instructions on page 76. To make a quilt, cut the number of pieces required following the cutting chart.

Block Size: 16" × 16" (41cm × 41cm)

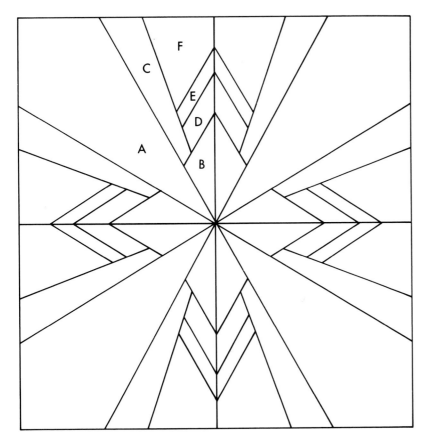

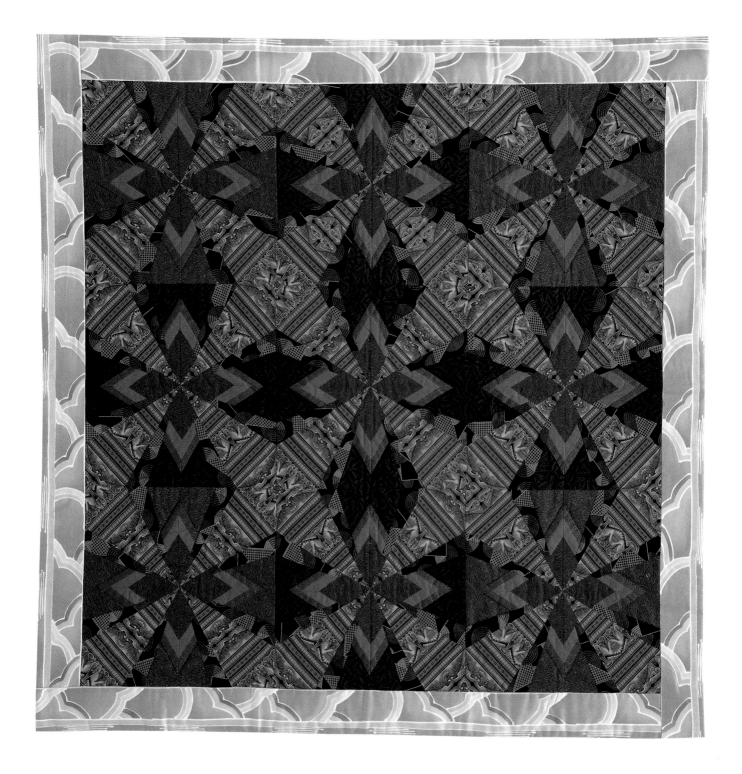

SPACE CENTER : *Quilt*

	WALL/CRIB	TWIN	DOUBLE/QUEEN	KING
Size (inches)	55 × 55	71 × 87	87 × 87	103 × 103
Size (centimeters)	140 × 140	180 × 221	221 × 221	262 × 262
Setting	3 × 3	4 × 5	5 × 5	6 × 6
Blocks	9	20	25	36

Fabric needed: *Yards (centimeters) for 45" (114cm) fabric*

Template A	1½ (140)	3¼ (300)	4 (370)	5¾ (520)
Template B	¾ (60)	1¼ (110)	1½ (140)	2⅛ (190)
Template C	⅞ (80)	1⅞ (170)	2⅜ (210)	3¼ (300)
Template D	½ (40)	⅞ (80)	1 (90)	1½ (130)
Template E	⅜ (30)	⅝ (50)	¾ (60)	⅞ (80)
Template F	⅞ (80)	2 (180)	2½ (220)	3⅜ (310)
Border: 4" (10cm)	1¾ (150)	2½ (230)	2½ (230)	3⅛ (280)

Cutting

Template A	36	80	100	144
Template B	72	160	200	288
Template C	72	160	200	288
Template D	72	160	200	288
Template E	72	160	200	288
Template F	72	160	200	288

Border width is 4" (10cm) including ¼" (6mm) seam allowance.

1.

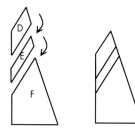

2.

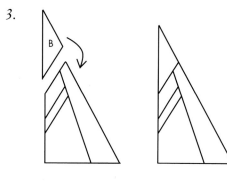

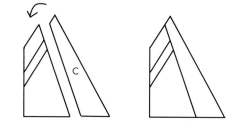

3.

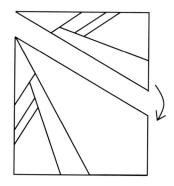

4.

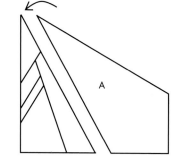 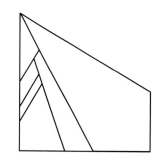

ASSEMBLY INSTRUCTIONS

To assemble each block, sew the pieces together in the following sequence, using the step-by-step drawings and the diagram as a guide.

1. Sew piece D to E, and E to piece F.
2. Sew piece C to no. 1.
3. Sew piece B to no. 2.
4. Sew piece A to no. 3.
5. Repeat steps 1–4 with a reverse set of pieces and sew this to no. 4, forming a quarter-block.
6. Repeat steps 1–5 to form a total of 4 quarter-blocks; sew the quarter-blocks together to complete the block.

If you are making a quilt, assemble and sew together the number of blocks required to complete your project. For example, the quilt shown here is wall hanging size, with nine blocks sewn in 3 rows of 3 blocks each, plus a border.

5.

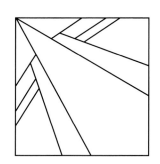

6.

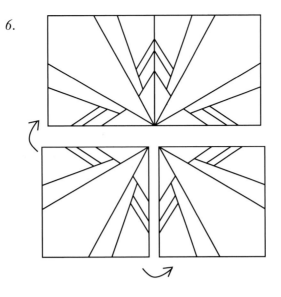

EGYPTIAN

There will be a feast at the pharaoh's palace in celebration of a newborn baby. Hunters bring back an abundance of game, and servants prepare a variety of fresh fruits. Fragrant flowers and expensive wines on the table await the guests who arrive in a steady stream. With a fanfare, the pharaoh and the mistress appear in the banquet room wearing dazzling jewels and crowns. Beautiful dancers wearing veils are waiting in the next room, ready to perform their best. The feast is about to begin.

INSTRUCTIONS

Cut the required number of fabric pieces as indicated on the templates on page 161. To assemble the block, sew the pieces together in the following sequence, using the diagram as a guide. This block is made of 4 quarter-blocks.

1. Sew piece A to piece B, forming a pyramid.
2. Sew 2 C pieces to no. 1.
3. Sew piece F to no. 2, forming a pyramid quarter-block.
4. Repeat steps 1–3 to form 2 quarter-blocks.
5. Sew the D pieces together in 2 strips of 5 each.
6. Sew one E piece to each no. 5 to form 2 quarter-blocks.
7. Sew the quarter-blocks together to complete the block.

Block size: 16" × 16" (41cm × 41cm)

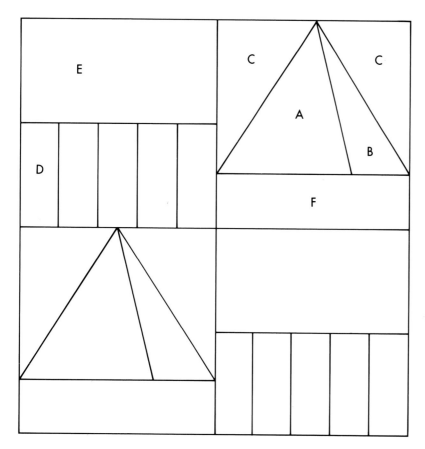

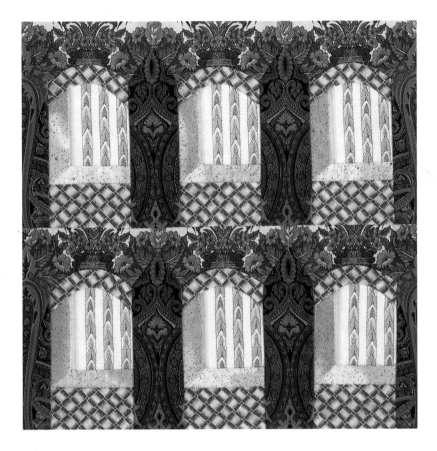

PERGOLA

A Spanish-style pergola encloses a house on a hill with beautiful climbing roses. The sun setting behind the house dyes the white lattice red, and the deepening shadows darken the wooden supports. A day of blooming is almost over, and the roses require an evening of rest and water so that they can enhance the environment again tomorrow.

INSTRUCTIONS

Cut the required number of fabric pieces as indicated on the templates on page 163. To assemble the block, sew the pieces together in the following sequence, using the diagram as a guide.

1. Sew 1 B piece and 1 C piece to 1 A piece; repeat to form 6 units.
2. Sew the D and E pieces to the no. 1 units.
3. Appliqué the no. 2 units onto the F pieces.
4. Sew the G pieces to the no. 3 units using the diagram as a guide.
5. Sew 1 H piece to each of the 4 remaining no. 3 units.
6. Sew the units together in 2 rows of 3 to complete the block.

Block size: 16″ × 16″ (41cm × 41cm)

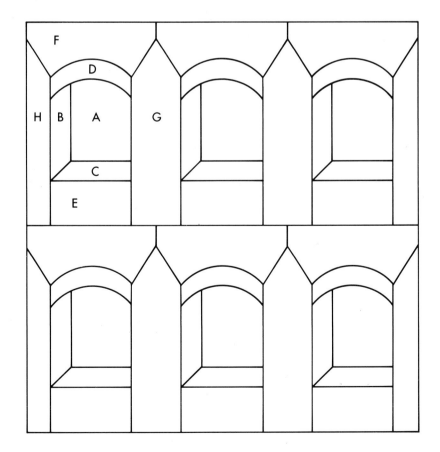

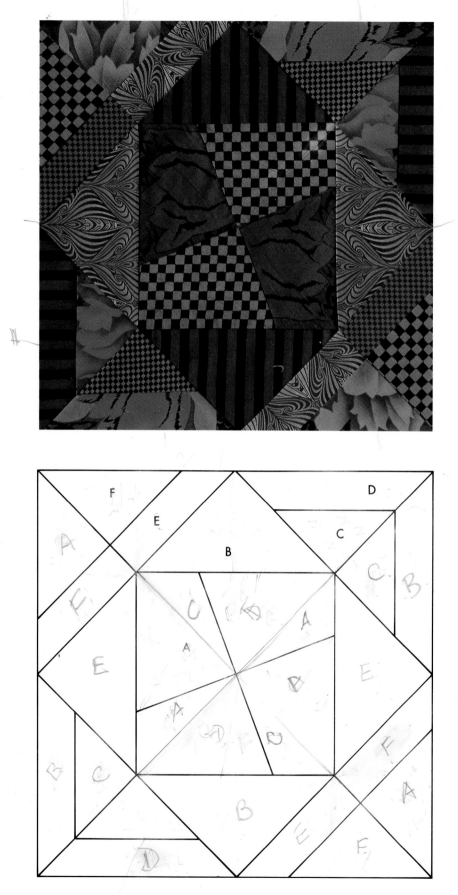

CADILLAC

The word Cadillac *is synonymous with America itself. The car is admired by everyone in the world because of its chic and debonair styling. I imagine the owners of the car to be a gentleman in a tuxedo with a red carnation and a lady with her hair cut in a bob, holding a long cigarette holder and wearing an elegant diamond ring. A capped chauffeur with a professional manner steps on the gas and glides smoothly down Fifth Avenue.*

INSTRUCTIONS

Cut the required number of fabric pieces as indicated on the templates on page 164. To assemble the block, sew the pieces together in the following sequence, using the diagram as a guide.

1. Sew 4 A pieces together.
2. Sew 4 B pieces to no. 1.
3. Sew 1 C piece to 1 D piece; repeat to form 4 triangles.
4. Sew the no. 3 units together in pairs.
5. Sew 1 E piece to 1 F piece; repeat to form 4 triangles.
6. Sew the 4 no. 5 units together in pairs.
7. Sew units no. 4 and 6 to no. 2 to complete the block.

Block size: 16″ × 16″ (41cm × 41cm)

CHARLESTON

The red striped dress with long fringes sways to and fro on the checkerboard linoleum floor. A green scarf wrapped around the waist dances to the tune of the Charleston played by the big band on the semicircular stage. On a nearby banquet table stands a large bouquet of roses, and behind the bat-wing doors people are betting on roulette.

INSTRUCTIONS

Cut the required number of fabric pieces as indicated on the templates on page 166. To assemble the block, sew the pieces together in the following sequence, using the diagram as a guide. This block is made of 4 quarter-blocks.

1. Appliqué piece A to piece B.
2. Sew 2 C pieces to no. 1.
3. Appliqué piece E onto piece D.
4. Appliqué no. 3 onto no. 2.
5. Appliqué no. 4 onto piece G.
6. Appliqué no. 5 onto piece F.
7. Repeat steps 1–6 to form a total of 4 quarter-blocks.
8. Sew the 4 quarter-blocks together to complete the block.

Block size: 16" × 16" (41cm × 41cm)

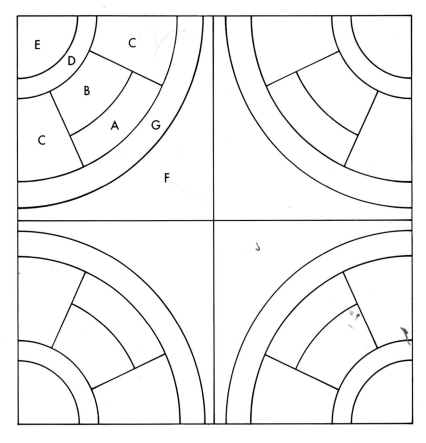

HUNTING PARTY

Gentlemen in red blazers and black derby hats are ready for fox hunting, each one mounted on his favorite horse. As they discuss the day's strategy, the beagles and dalmatians make a great noise as if already scenting the smell of foxes. On the signal of the host, the whole hunting party and the dogs swiftly disappear into the woods.

INSTRUCTIONS

Cut the required number of fabric pieces as indicated on the templates on page 167. To assemble the block, sew the pieces together in the following sequence, using the diagram as a guide.

1. Sew piece A to piece B to form a triangle.
2. Sew 2 D pieces to a C piece.
3. Sew no. 1 to no. 2 to form a larger triangle.
4. Repeat steps 1–3 to form a total of 4 triangular units.
5. Sew the 4 pieced triangular units together to form the square center unit.
6. Sew an E piece to an F piece; repeat to form a total of 8 triangular units.
7. Sew 2 F pieces to each G piece to form a total of 24 parallelograms.
8. Sew the 24 parallelograms together in 4 rows of 6.
9. Sew a no. 6 triangular unit to each end of the no. 8 row units, forming rectangular pieces.
10. Sew a no. 9 unit to the top and bottom edges of the square center unit.
11. Sew 1 H piece to each end of the 2 remaining no. 9 units.
12. Sew the no. 11 units to the sides of the center unit to complete the block.

Block size: 15 ½" × 15 ½" (39.5 × 39.5 cm)

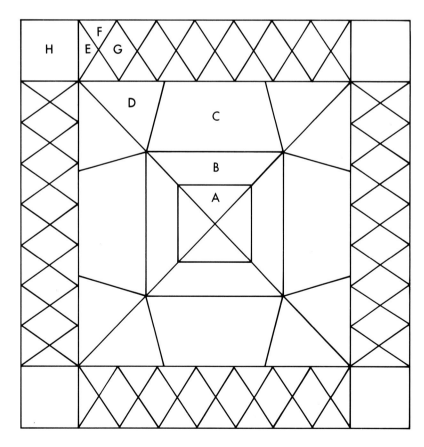

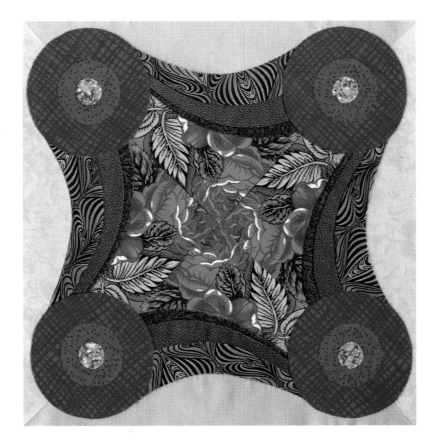

ROSE GARDEN

Four marble columns tower over the blue Mediterranean Sea. The garden's sculptured hedges and trees sway like twisted swags, embracing the columns. Roses in many colors are at their best and emit their fragrance into the atmosphere, like little angels emerging from the heavens.

CUTTING INSTRUCTIONS

To make one block, cut the required number of pieces indicated on the templates on page 169. To assemble the block, see assembly instructions on page 86. To make a quilt, cut the number of pieces required following the cutting chart, including the lattice strips and squares (chart measurements include ¼" [6mm] seam allowance).

Block Size: 16" × 16" (41cm × 41cm)

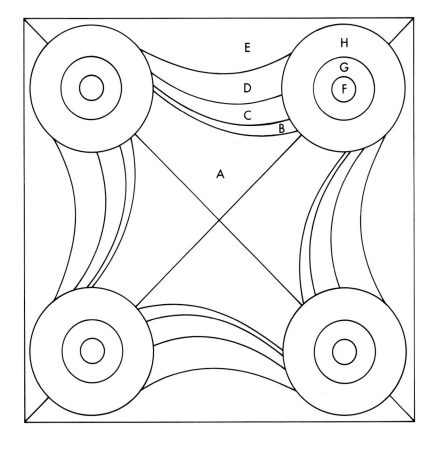

ROSE GARDEN : *Quilt*

	WALL/CRIB	TWIN	DOUBLE/QUEEN	KING
Size (inches)	46.5 × 46.5	65 × 83.5	83.5 × 102	102 × 102
Size (centimeters)	118 × 118	171 × 212	212 × 259	259 × 259
Setting	2 × 2	3 × 4	4 × 5	5 × 5
Blocks	4	12	20	25

Fabric needed: Yards (centimeters) for 45" (114cm) fabric

Template A	⅝ (50)	1½ (130)	2⅜ (210)	2⅞ (260)
Template B	¼ (20)	⅝ (50)	⅞ (80)	1 (90)
Template C	¼ (20)	⅝ (50)	⅞ (80)	1⅛ (100)
Template D	¼ (20)	¾ (60)	1 (90)	1⅛ (100)
Template E	¾ (60)	1¾ (150)	2¾ (250)	3⅜ (310)
Template F	¼ (20)	¼ (20)	⅜ (30)	⅜ (30)
Template G	¼ (20)	½ (40)	¾ (60)	⅞ (80)
Template H	½ (40)	1⅛ (100)	1¾ (160)	2⅛ (190)
Lattice strips: 3" (8cm)	¾ (60)	1½ (130)	2⅜ (200)	2¾ (240)
Lattice squares: 3" (8cm)	¼ (20)	⅜ (30)	⅜ (30)	⅜ (30)
Border: 4" (10cm)	1½ (130)	2½ (220)	3 (270)	3 (270)

Cutting

Template A	16	48	80	100
Template B	16	48	80	100
Template C	16	48	80	100
Template D	16	48	80	100
Template E	16	48	80	100
Template F	16	48	80	100
Template G	16	48	80	100
Template H	16	48	80	100

	WALL/CRIB	TWIN	DOUBLE/QUEEN	KING
Lattice strips 16½" × 3" *(42cm × 8cm)*	12	31	49	60
Lattice squares 3" × 3" *(8cm × 8cm)*	9	20	30	36

Border width is 4" (10cm) including ¼" (6mm) seam allowance.

1.

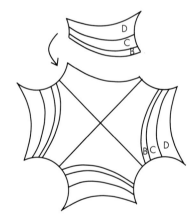

2.

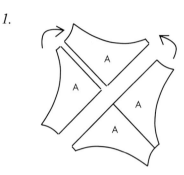

ASSEMBLY INSTRUCTIONS

To assemble each block, sew the pieces together in the following sequence, using the step-by-step drawings and the diagram as a guide.

1. Sew 4 A pieces together.
2. Appliqué 4 B, C, and D pieces onto no. 1.
3. Appliqué 4 E pieces onto no. 2.
4. Appliqué the 4 F pieces onto the 4 G pieces and the G pieces onto the H pieces.
5. Appliqué the no. 4 units onto no. 3 to complete the block.

If you are making a quilt, sew the number of blocks required to complete your project. For example, the quilt shown here is wall hanging size, with 4 blocks sewn in 2 rows of 2 blocks each. Following the diagram, sew the blocks, lattice strips, and lattice squares together, and then add the outside border.

3.

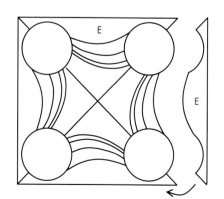

4.

5.

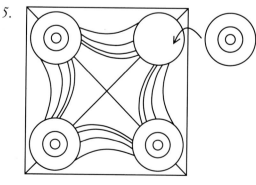

AQUARIUM

It is a pleasant experience to visit an aquarium by the sea. Behind huge glass walls we find all kinds of fish, sea shells, and sea weed — some of which we have never seen before. The most interesting creatures in the marine world are the sea otters; they seem so lovable when they somersault and when they crack open abalone on their stomachs. The only thing we missed that day at the aquarium was a mermaid!

INSTRUCTIONS

Cut the required number of fabric pieces as indicated on the templates on page 171. To assemble the block, sew the pieces together as follows, using the diagram as a guide.

1. Appliqué 1 B piece onto each of 2 A pieces.
2. Sew 1 E to each no. 1 along the B seam.
3. Appliqué 1 D piece onto each of 2 F pieces.
4. Sew each no. 3 to a C piece.
5. Sew each no. 2 to a no. 4, forming 2 quarter-circles.
6. Appliqué one D piece onto each of the remaining C pieces.
7. Sew each no. 6 unit to an F piece.
8. Appliqué 1 B onto each of the remaining E pieces.
9. Sew each no. 8 to an A piece.
10. Sew each no. 7 to a no. 9, forming 2 quarter-circles.
11. Sew each of the no. 5 quarter-circles to one of the no. 10 quarter-circles, forming 2 half-circles.
12. Sew the two half-circles together.
13. Sew the G pieces to the corners of no. 12.
14. Appliqué the H pieces to the sides of the circle to complete the block.

Block size: 16″ × 16″ (41cm × 41cm)

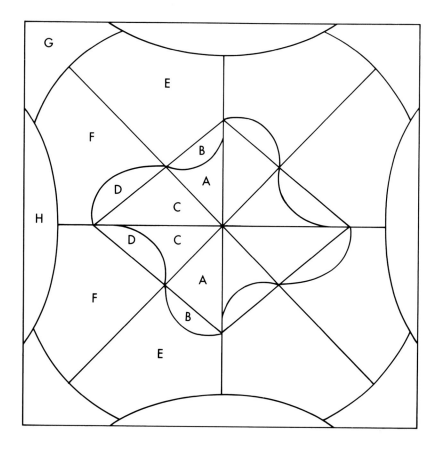

CAROUSEL

The autumn fair has come to a small farming town. Children pet the donkeys, horses, pigs and goats. A variety of stalls sell cotton candy, candied apples, ice cream, and juicy watermelons. The clock mounted at the top of the City Hall chimes three o'clock, and school children burst out of the class rooms and run to the carousel with glee. Can you hear? Lively music is everywhere.

INSTRUCTIONS

Cut the required number of fabric pieces as indicated on the templates on page 173. To assemble the block, sew the pieces together in the following sequence, using the diagram as a guide. This block is made of 4 quarter-blocks.

1. Appliqué piece A onto piece B.
2. Sew piece C to piece D.
3. Appliqué no. 1 onto no. 2.
4. Appliqué a second piece A onto no. 3.
5. Repeat steps 1–4 to form a total of 4 quarter-blocks.
6. Sew the quarter-blocks together to complete the block.

Block size: 16" × 16" (41cm × 41cm)

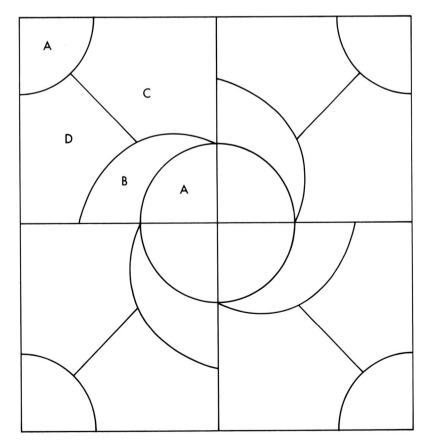

CAMELLIA

Snow has fallen on the rink overnight. Despite the cold winter afternoon, children enjoy skating on the ice. Cold wind whistling through the air inflates a girl's red cape like a camellia, with a yellow muff as the core of the flower.

INSTRUCTIONS

Cut the required number of fabric pieces as indicated on the templates on page 175. To assemble the block, sew the pieces together in the following sequence, using the diagram as a guide. This block is made of 9 pieced squares first sewn into 3 rows.

1. Appliqué piece B onto A, and then appliqué piece C onto B; repeat to form a total of 4 pieced squares.
2. Sew G to H; repeat to form a total of 4 pieced triangles.
3. Sew E to F; repeat to form 4 pieced triangles.
4. Sew the 4 no. 2 units to the 4 no. 3 units, forming a total of 4 pieced squares.
5. Sew the 4 D pieces together to form the center square.
6. Sew the squares into 3 rows, following the diagram.
7. Sew the 3 rows together to complete the block.

Block size: 16″ × 16″ (41cm × 41cm)

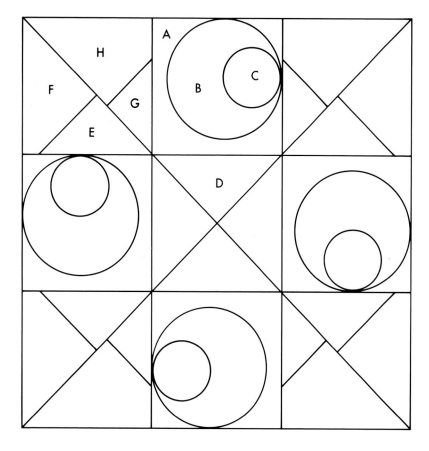

KABUKI

Classical Theatrical Play

Kabuki is a Japanese classical theatrical play and is famous for its spectacular revolving stage, gorgeous costumes and women impersonators. Their makeup uses circles and triangles to represent different facial expressions. The color red usually represents the female role and black represents the male. In this design, the square shapes in beige represent the drop curtain of the Kabuki stage.

INSTRUCTIONS

Cut the required number of fabric pieces as indicated on the templates on page 177. To assemble the block, sew the pieces together in the following sequence, using the diagram as a guide.

1. Make 3 rows of 3 A pieces each.
2. Sew the 3 rows together, forming the square background of the block.
3. Appliqué the two E pieces onto the background square.
4. Appliqué the B pieces onto the background square, sewing along the edges of the E pieces.
5. Appliqué the C pieces onto the B pieces, sewing along the edges of the E pieces.
6. Appliqué the D pieces onto the B pieces, sewing along the edges of the E pieces.

Block size: 16" × 16" (41cm × 41cm)

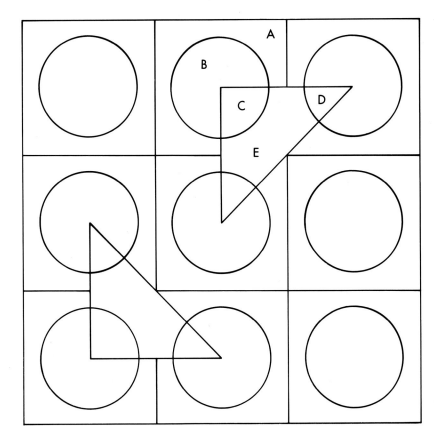

ELECTRIC FAN

A four-winged wooden fan on the ceiling rotates leisurely in the summer afternoon. Underneath, southern belles are busily gossiping while playing chess. Behind maroon colored divans children play a game of hide-and-seek. As the sweet smell of magnolia blossoms slips into the room, the ladies enjoy homemade lemonade.

INSTRUCTIONS

Cut the required number of fabric pieces as indicated on the templates on page 179. To assemble the block, sew the pieces together in the following sequence, using the diagram as a guide.

1. Appliqué piece B onto piece A.
2. Sew piece C to no. 1.
3. Appliqué piece D onto no. 2.
4. Appliqué 2 E pieces onto no. 3.
5. Repeat steps 1–4 to form a total of 4 units.
6. Sew the no. 5 units together.
7. Appliqué the 4 F pieces onto the sides of no. 6.
8. Appliqué piece G to no. 7.

Block size: 16" × 16" (41cm × 41cm)

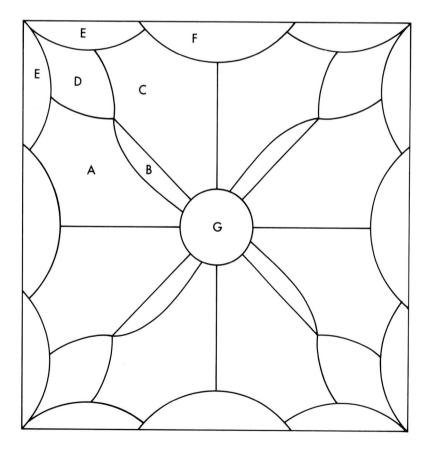

SCOTTISH THISTLE

The morning sunlight filters through the small window, illuminating Ann Boleyn's pale face. She has been confined behind the stone walls for quite some time, and her only comfort is the view of Scottish thistles blooming over the hill in the direction of her native land where she longs to return some-day. She is only twenty-three years old.

CUTTING INSTRUCTIONS

To make one block, cut the required number of pieces indicated on the templates on page 181. To assemble the block, see assembly instructions on page 96. To make a quilt, cut the number of pieces required following the cutting chart.

Block Size: 16" × 16" (41cm × 41cm)

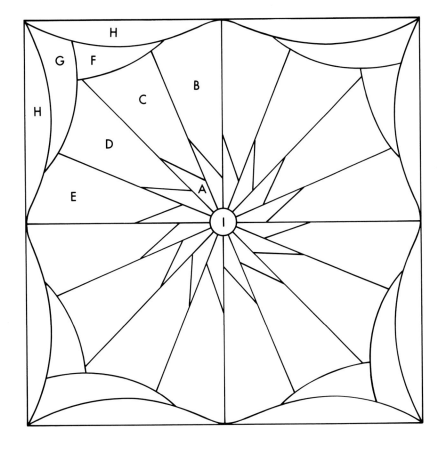

SCOTTISH THISTLE : *Quilt*

	WALL/CRIB	TWIN	DOUBLE/QUEEN	KING
Size (inches)	36 × 52	68 × 84	84 × 84	100 × 100
Size (centimeters)	91 × 132	173 × 213	213 × 213	254 × 254
Setting	2 × 3	4 × 5	5 × 5	6 × 6
Blocks	6	20	25	36

Fabric needed: Yards (centimeters) for 45" (114cm) fabric

	WALL/CRIB	TWIN	DOUBLE/QUEEN	KING
Template A	⅝ (50)	1¾ (160)	2⅛ (190)	3 (270)
Template B	½ (40)	1⅜ (120)	1¾ (150)	2⅜ (210)
Template C	½ (40)	1⅜ (120)	1¾ (150)	2⅜ (210)
Template D	½ (40)	1⅜ (120)	1¾ (150)	2⅜ (210)
Template E	½ (40)	1⅜ (120)	1¾ (150)	2⅜ (210)
Template F	⅜ (30)	⅞ (80)	1 (90)	1½ (130)
Template G	⅜ (30)	1 (90)	1⅛ (110)	1⅝ (150)
Template H	⅞ (80)	2⅜ (210)	2⅞ (260)	4¼ (380)
Template I	¼ (20)	¼ (20)	¼ (20)	¼ (20)
Border: 2½" (6cm)	1½ (140)	2½ (220)	2½ (220)	3 (290)

Cutting

	WALL/CRIB	TWIN	DOUBLE/QUEEN	KING
Template A	96	320	400	576
Template B	24	80	100	156
Template C	24	80	100	156
Template D	24	80	100	156
Template E	24	80	100	156
Template F	24	80	100	156
Template G	24	80	100	156
Template H	48	160	200	312
Template I	6	20	25	36

Border width is 2½" (6mm) including ¼" (6mm) seam allowance.

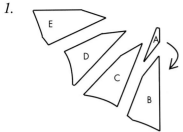

1.

2.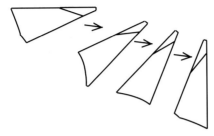

3.

4.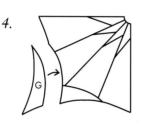

5.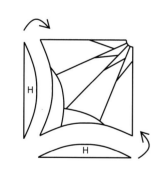

6. & 7.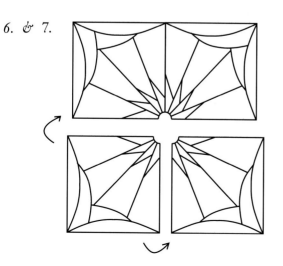

ASSEMBLY INSTRUCTIONS

To assemble each block, sew the pieces together in the following sequence, using the step-by-step drawings and the diagram as a guide.

1. Sew 1 piece A to each piece B, C, D, and E.
2. Sew B, C, D, and E together.
3. Appliqué piece F onto no. 2.
4. Appliqué piece G onto no. 3.
5. Appliqué two H pieces onto no. 4, forming a quarter-block.
6. Repeat steps 1–5 to form a total of 4 quarter-blocks.
7. Sew the 4 quarter-blocks together.
8. Appliqué piece I onto no. 7 to complete the block.

If you are making a quilt, assemble and sew together the number of blocks required to complete your project. For example, the quilt shown here is wall hanging size, with six blocks sewn in two rows of three, plus a border.

8.

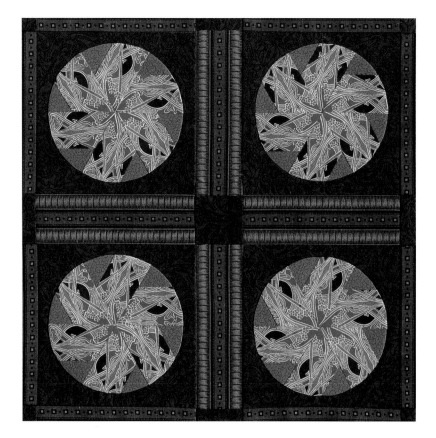

BRILLIANT CUT

A woman in a red dress gazes longingly into the window of Tiffany's on Fifth Avenue. Her eyes are fixed on a large diamond solitaire with many facets lying on purple velvet. The woman must have fallen into a magic spell at the sight of the jewel, because she and her red dress are now reflected inside the diamond. The brilliantly cut diamond becomes more luminous, enticing another woman in a blue dress, to peer into the store window.

INSTRUCTIONS

Cut the required number of fabric pieces as indicated on the templates on page 183. To assemble the block, sew the pieces together in the following sequence, using the diagram as a guide.

1. Sew 1 A piece to each B piece, forming 24 wedge-shaped units.
2. Sew 6 no. 1 wedges together, forming a circle; repeat to form a total of 6 circles.
3. Appliqué 1 no. 2 circle onto each C piece.
4. Sew 1 F piece to the side of each of 2 no. 3 units.
5. Sew 1 of each of the remaining no. 3's to each no. 4, forming 2 strips.
6. Make the center connecting strip by sewing the remaining F pieces to H.
7. Sew the no. 6 strip to the no. 5 strips.
8. Make 4 border strips by sewing one G to each D; then add an E to each end of 2 of the strips.
9. Sew the shorter strips to the sides of the block, then sew the longer strips to the top and bottom.

Block size: 15" × 15" (38cm × 38cm)

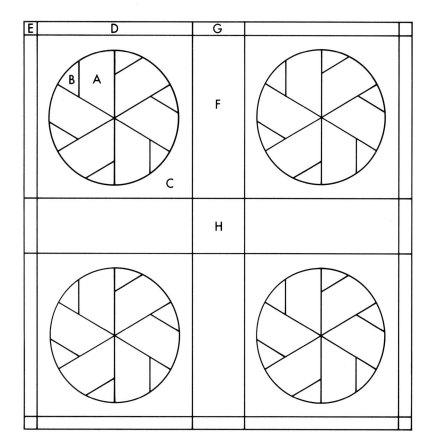

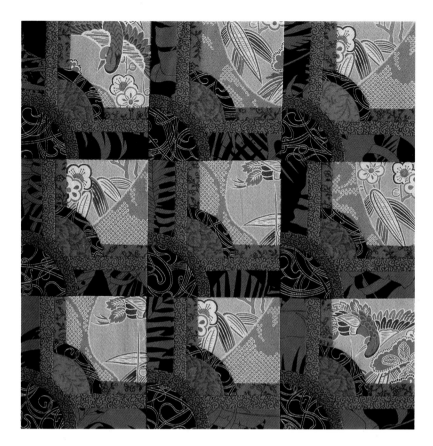

O-SHOGATSU お正月

New Year's Day

The observation of the New Year is most important in Japan, and many rituals take place during this period. The people worship as symbols of longevity the rising sun at dawn, cranes, pine and bamboo trees, and flowering plum blossoms. In this design I have arranged straight lines and curves of various sizes to create the effect of the sun about to rise on the icy winter morning.

INSTRUCTIONS

Cut the required number of fabric pieces as indicated on the templates on page 184. To assemble the block, sew the pieces together in the following sequence, using the diagram as a guide. This block is made of 9 square units first sewn together in 3 rows.

1. Sew 2 B pieces to an A piece.
2. Appliqué piece C onto no. 1.
3. Appliqué piece D onto no. 2.
4. Sew 2 E pieces onto no. 3.
5. Sew 2 F pieces onto no. 4.
6. Appliqué piece G onto no. 5.
7. Appliqué piece H onto no. 6.
8. Repeat steps 1–7 to make a total of 9 square units.
9. Sew the squares together in 3 rows of 3 squares each.
10. Sew the rows together, completing the block.

Block size: 16" × 16" (41cm × 41cm)

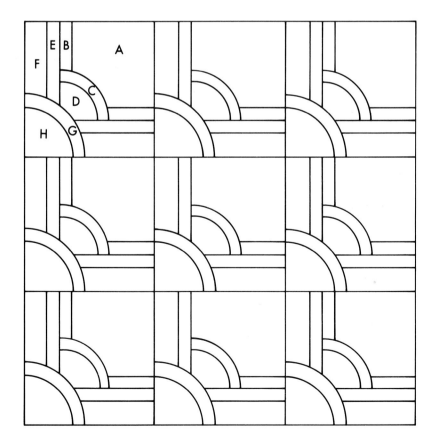

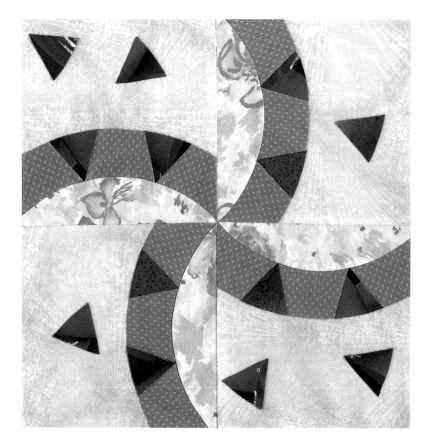

WAYWARD WIND

In early spring, when the air is still cold, a sudden turbulence surprises the people in the town. It causes all kinds of trouble and mischievously blows off a woman's hat and lifts a small packet from her hands into the air. Children chase a ball rolling down the slope and a little puppy loses its way in a strong puff of wind. The whole town is in a disheveled state for a few hours, thanks to the wayward wind.

INSTRUCTIONS

Cut the required number of fabric pieces as indicated on the templates on page 186. To assemble the block, sew the pieces together in the following sequence, using the diagram as a guide. This block is made of 4 quarter-blocks.

1. Sew piece A to piece B.
2. Sew piece C to another B piece.
3. Sew no. 1 and no. 2 together, forming an arc.
4. Sew piece D to the no. 3 arc.
5. Appliqué piece E onto no. 4.
6. Appliqué piece F to no. 5, forming a quarter-block.
7. Repeat steps 1–6 to form a total of 4 quarter-blocks.
8. Sew the quarter-blocks together.
9. Randomly appliqué 6 B pieces onto the F pieces to complete the block.

Block size: 16″ × 16″ (41cm × 41cm)

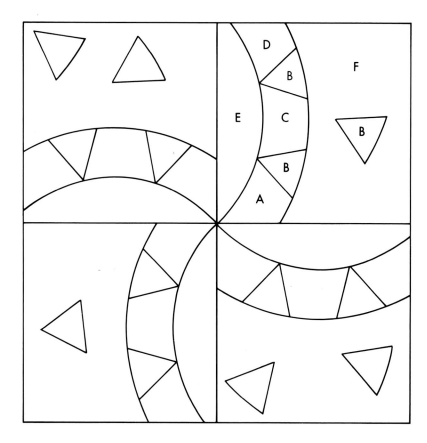

ROMANESQUE

Romanesque, characterized by heavy construction with round arches and vaulted ceilings, was the style of architecture prevalent in southern Europe from the ninth through the thirteenth centuries. The main source of the inspiration for this style was the Benedictine Abbey at Cluny in France; today some buildings remain only as ruins. The fallen pillars represented in this block are embraced by a massive growth of ivy and blooming primroses add their own colorful beauty to the long-decayed monastery.

CUTTING INSTRUCTIONS

To make one block, cut the required number of pieces indicated on the templates on page 187. To assemble the block, see assembly instructions on page 104. To make a quilt, cut the number of pieces required following the cutting chart.

Block size: 16″ × 16″ (41cm × 41cm)

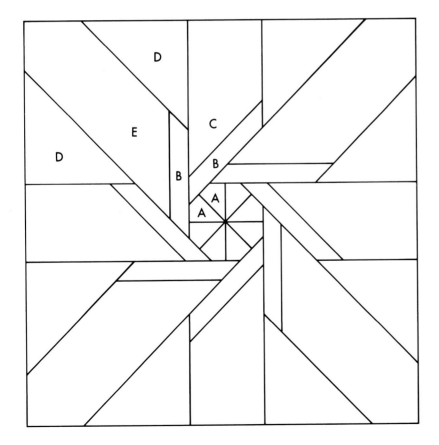

ROMANESQUE : *Quilt*

	WALL/CRIB	TWIN	DOUBLE/QUEEN	KING
Size (inches)	42 × 58	74 × 90	90 × 90	106 × 106
Size (centimeters)	107 × 147	188 × 229	229 × 229	269 × 269
Setting	2 × 3	4 × 5	5 × 5	6 × 6
Blocks	6	20	25	36

Fabric needed: Yards (centimeters) for 45" (114cm) fabric

	WALL/CRIB	TWIN	DOUBLE/QUEEN	KING
Template A	⅜ (30)	¾ (60)	⅞ (70)	1⅛ (100)
Template B	½ (40)	1 (90)	1¼ (110)	1⅝ (150)
Template C	½ (40)	1½ (130)	1¾ (160)	2½ (220)
Template D	¾ (60)	1¾ (160)	2¼ (200)	3⅛ (280)
Template E	⅞ (80)	2⅜ (210)	2⅞ (260)	4¼ (380)
Border: 1½" (4cm)	¼ (20)	⅜ (30)	½ (40)	⅝ (50)
Border: 4½" (11cm)	1¾ (160)	2⅝ (240)	2⅝ (240)	3⅛ (280)

Cutting

	WALL/CRIB	TWIN	DOUBLE/QUEEN	KING
Template A	48	160	200	288
Template B	48	160	200	288
Template C	24	80	100	144
Template D	48	160	200	288
Template E	24	80	100	144

Inside border width is 1½" (4cm) including ¼" (6mm) seam allowance.
Outside border width is 4½" (11cm) including ¼" (6mm) seam allowance.

1.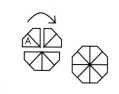

2.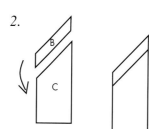

3.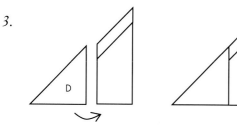

4.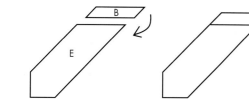

5.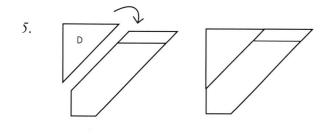

6.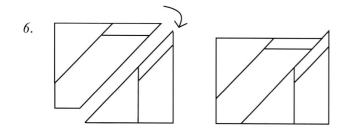

ASSEMBLY INSTRUCTIONS

To assemble each block, sew the pieces together in the following sequence, using the step-by-step drawings and the diagram as a guide.

1. Sew 8 A pieces together, forming the center unit.
2. Sew 1 B piece to each C piece.
3. Sew 1 D piece to each no. 2 unit to form 4 triangular units.
4. Sew 1 B piece to each E piece.
5. Sew 1 D piece to each no. 4 unit.
6. Sew the no. 3 and no. 5 units together along the diagonal seams, forming 4 quarter-blocks.
7. Sew the quarter-blocks together, using the diagram as a guide.
8. Appliqué the center unit onto the block.

If you are making a quilt, assemble and sew together the number of blocks required to complete your project. For example, the quilt shown here is wall hanging size, with six blocks sewn in 2 rows of 3 blocks each, plus an inside and outside border.

7.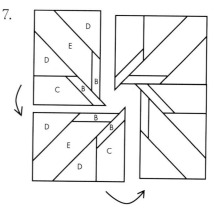

8.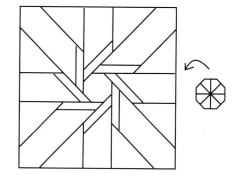

GENROKU

元禄

Genroku Period

The Genroku period in Japan from 1688–1704 was like the Renaissance in Europe; artistic movements bloomed in many directions and kimono designs were reborn with more gorgeous materials and shades. A checkerboard pattern came in with the period and stayed in vogue for many years to come. Combinations of floral and geometric designs such as the one I used here were also very much in fashion at that time.

INSTRUCTIONS

Cut the required number of fabric pieces as indicated on the templates on page 189. To assemble the block, sew the pieces together in the following sequence, using the diagram as a guide. The design consists of 4 quarter-blocks turned on end.

1. Appliqué piece B onto piece A.
2. Sew piece C to no. 1.
3. Appliqué piece B onto piece D.
4. Sew no. 2 and no. 3 together.
5. Sew piece E to no. 4.
6. Appliqué two B pieces onto piece F.
7. Sew no. 5 and no. 6 together to form a quarter-block.
8. Repeat steps 1–7 to form a total of 4 quarter-blocks.
9. Sew the quarter-blocks together, rotating them on end as shown in the diagram, to complete the block.

Block size: 16" × 16" (41cm × 41cm)

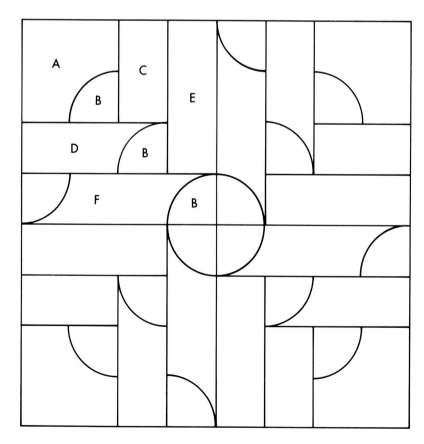

IKEGAKI

Bamboo Fence

Green and red rectangular shapes connected by small triangles suggest the structure of the bamboo lattice seen in many Japanese houses. The circles represent flowers blooming in an enclosed garden, which contrast with diagonal shapes, creating the illusion of perspective.

INSTRUCTIONS

Cut the required number of fabric pieces as indicated on the templates on page 191. To assemble the block, sew the pieces together in the following sequence, using the diagram as a guide.

1. Appliqué 1 B piece onto each corner of piece A.
2. Sew 4 D pieces together; repeat to form 4 square units.
3. Sew the no. 2 square units to the ends of 2 C pieces.
4. Sew the C pieces and no. 3 units to the sides of no. 1, forming the center unit.
5. Appliqué 1 B piece to each G piece, forming a triangular unit.
6. Appliqué the remaining B pieces to the F pieces.
7. Sew the E pieces to the no. 6 units.
8. Sew 2 no. 7 units to the no. 4 center unit.
9. Sew 2 no. 5 triangular units to a no. 7 unit, following the diagram; repeat to form 2 large triangular units.
10. Sew the no. 9 triangular units to the center unit to complete the block.

Block size: 15" × 15" (38cm × 38cm)

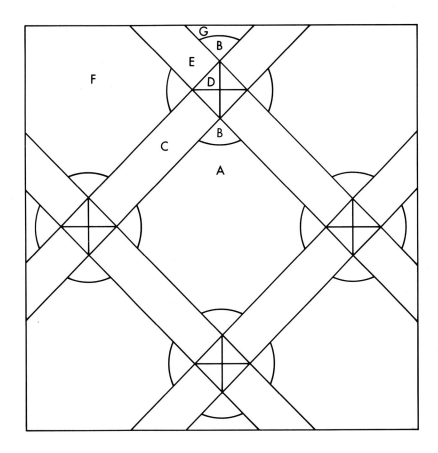

BACKYARD

The towering mass of clouds in the summer sky almost seems within arm's reach. The laundry on the clothesline flies high in the air, as if to greet the sky with a "Hello everybody!" On the green grass a mother nurses a newborn baby, and older children toss a ball back and forth. Everything seems peaceful and quiet, except for occasional laughter; apples on the tree have begun to turn red.

INSTRUCTIONS

Cut the required number of fabric pieces as indicated on the templates on page 193. To assemble the block, sew the pieces together in the following sequence, using the diagram as a guide.

1. Appliqué A, B, C, D, E, and F onto the background fabric.
2. Embroider the clothesline using an outline stitch and the clothespins using a satin stitch.

Block size: 16" × 16" (41cm × 41cm)

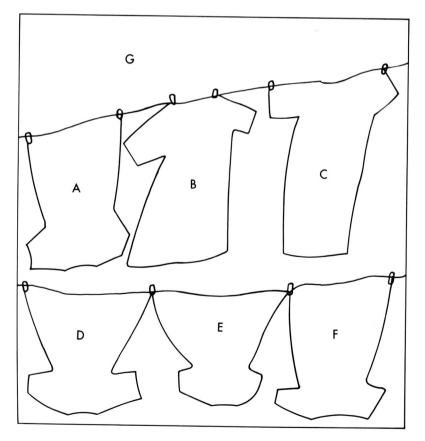

TEMPLATES

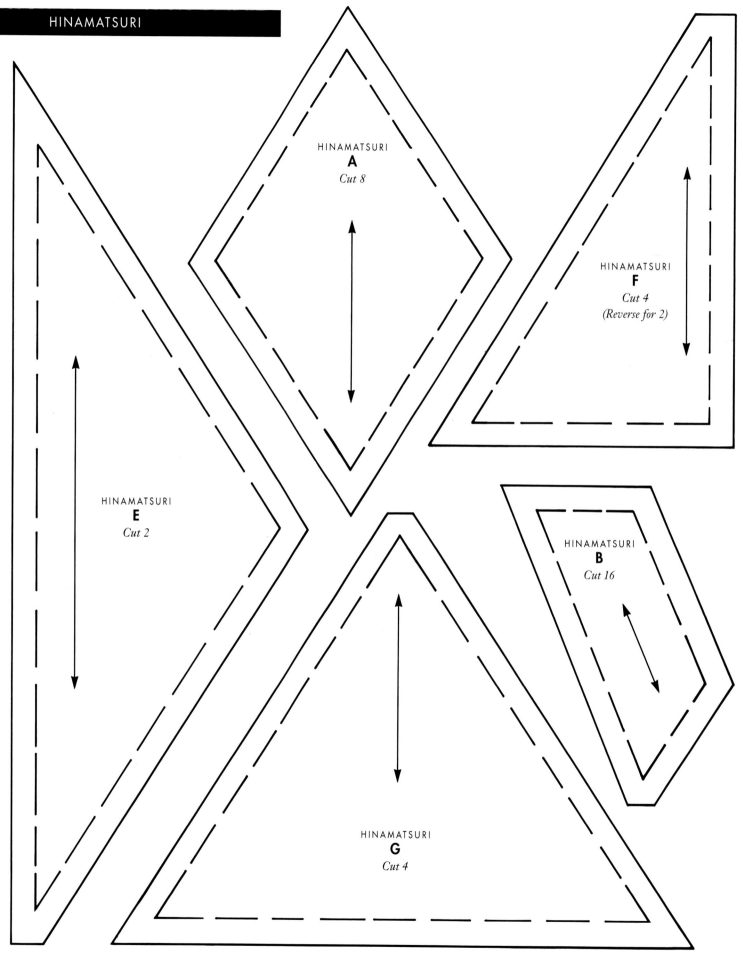

HINAMATSURI
A
Cut 8

HINAMATSURI
F
Cut 4
(Reverse for 2)

HINAMATSURI
E
Cut 2

HINAMATSURI
B
Cut 16

HINAMATSURI
G
Cut 4

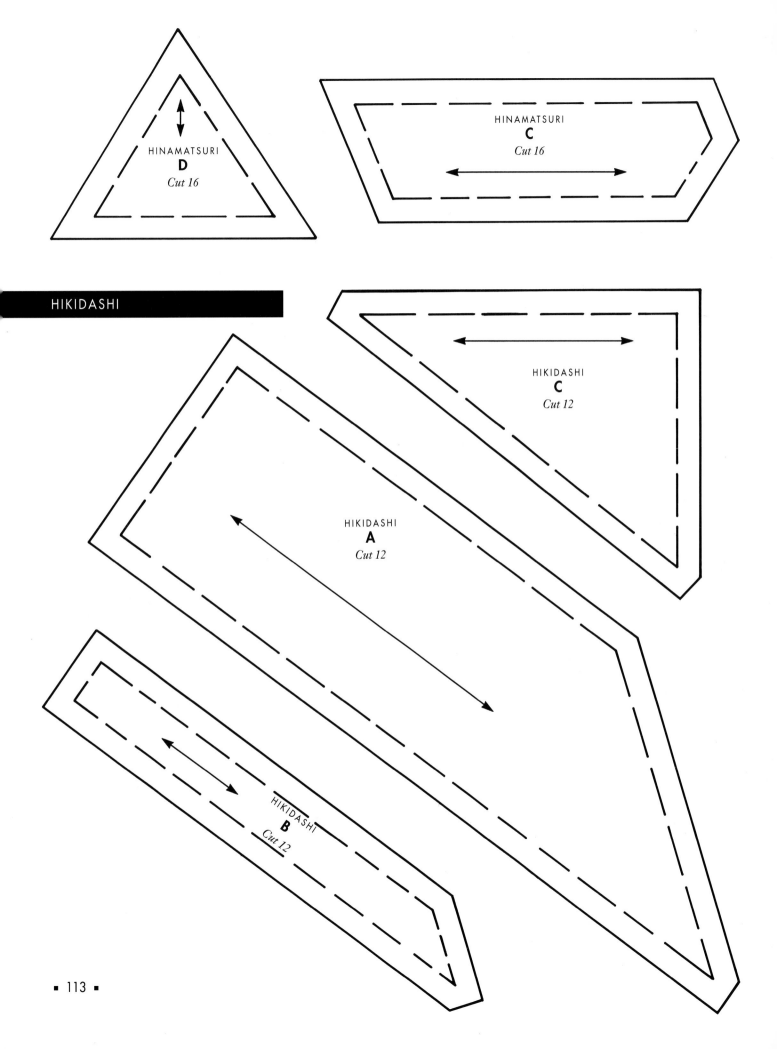

HINAMATSURI
D
Cut 16

HINAMATSURI
C
Cut 16

HIKIDASHI

HIKIDASHI
C
Cut 12

HIKIDASHI
A
Cut 12

HIKIDASHI
B
Cut 12

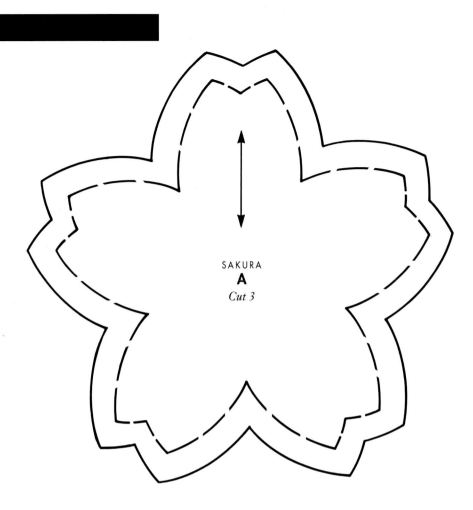

SAKURA
A
Cut 3

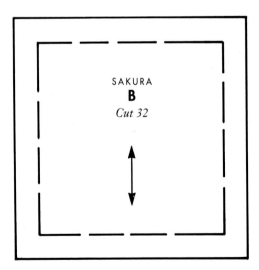

SAKURA
B
Cut 32

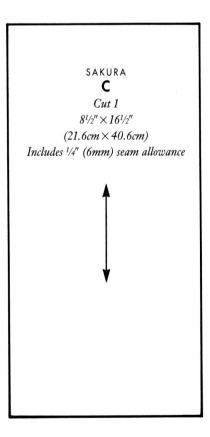

SAKURA
C
Cut 1
8½″ × 16½″
(21.6cm × 40.6cm)
Includes ¼″ (6mm) seam allowance

NOTE: *The templates indicate the number of pieces needed for making* **one block.** *To determine the number of pieces needed to make a complete quilt, refer to the cutting charts that accompany the quilt instructions.*

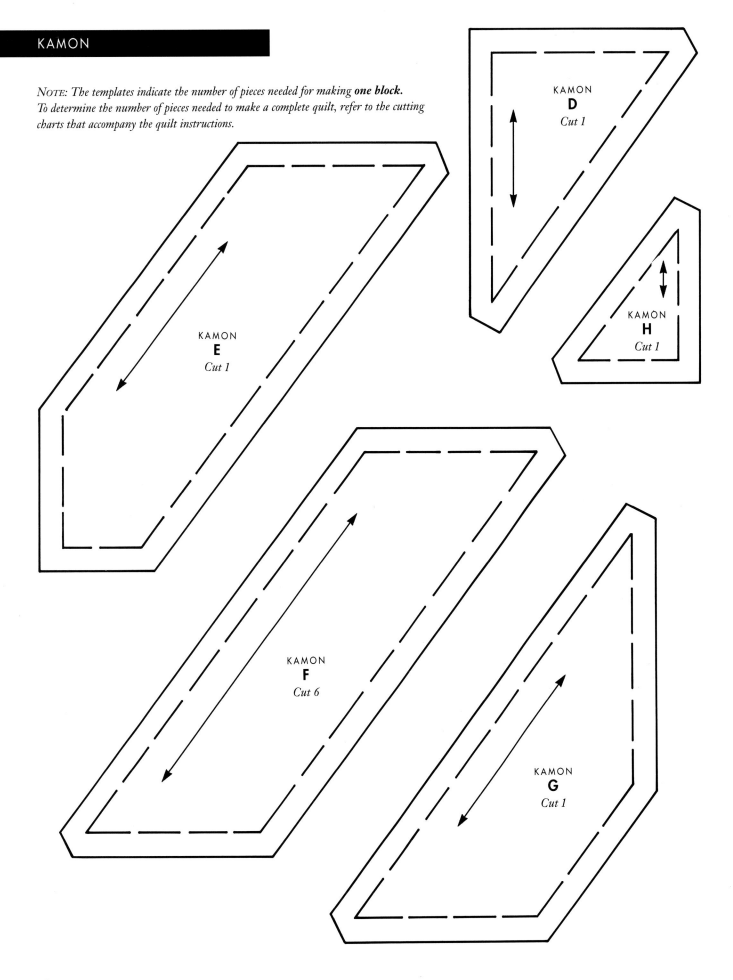

KAMON
D
Cut 1

KAMON
H
Cut 1

KAMON
E
Cut 1

KAMON
F
Cut 6

KAMON
G
Cut 1

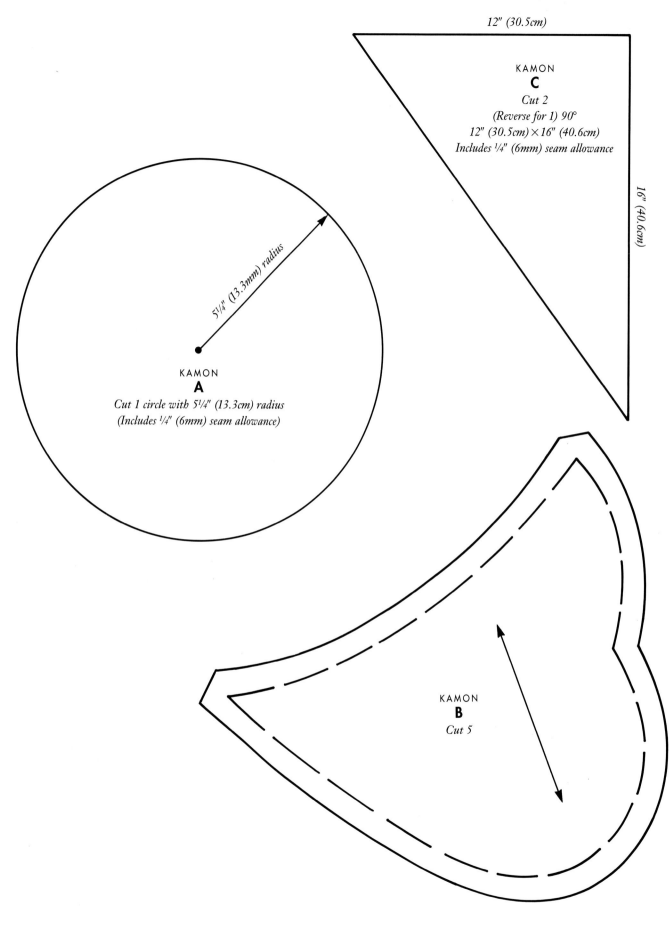

12" (30.5cm)

KAMON
C
Cut 2
(Reverse for 1) 90°
12" (30.5cm) × 16" (40.6cm)
Includes ¼" (6mm) seam allowance

16" (40.6cm)

5¼" (13.3mm) radius

KAMON
A
Cut 1 circle with 5¼" (13.3cm) radius
(Includes ¼" (6mm) seam allowance)

KAMON
B
Cut 5

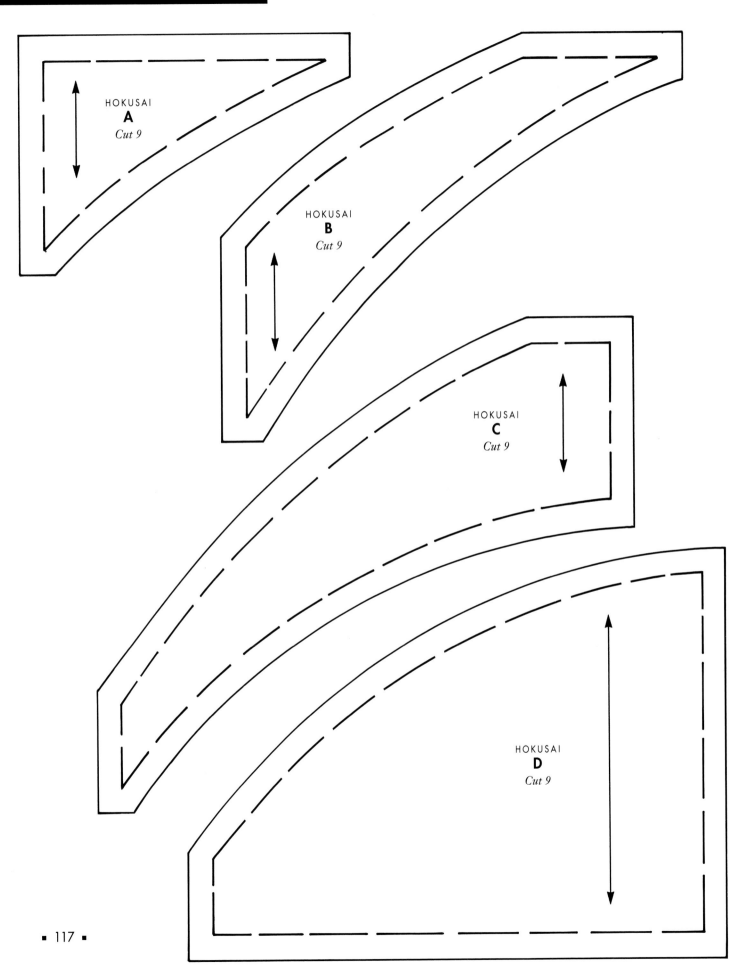

HOKUSAI
A
Cut 9

HOKUSAI
B
Cut 9

HOKUSAI
C
Cut 9

HOKUSAI
D
Cut 9

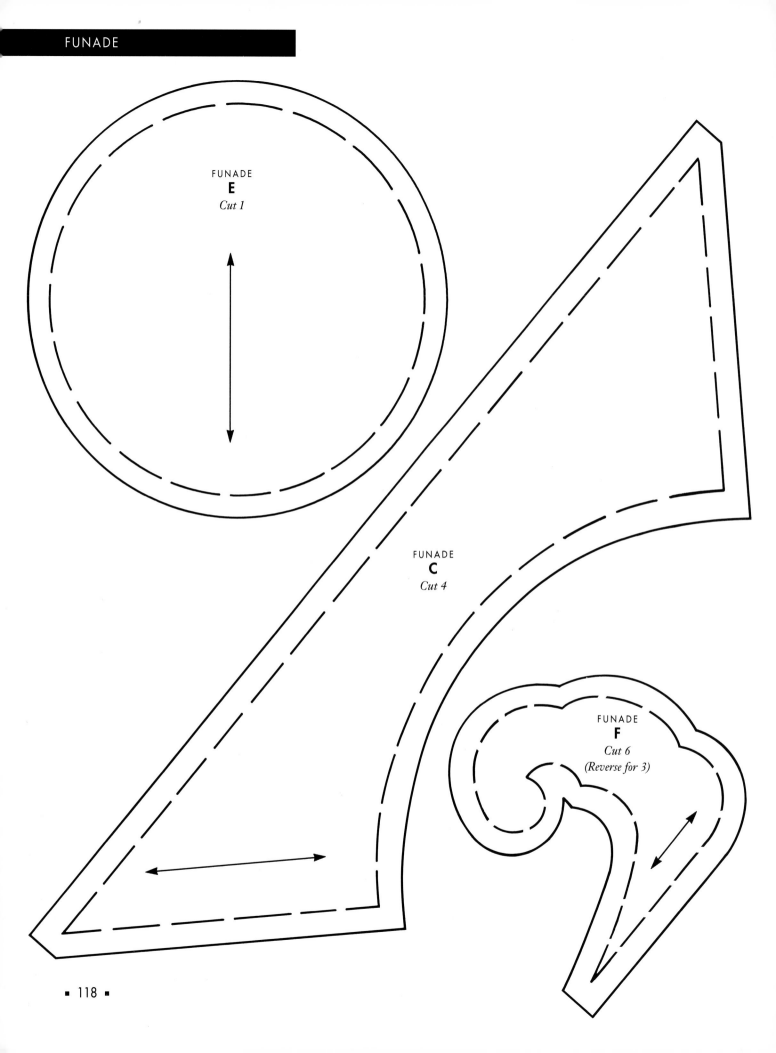

FUNADE
E
Cut 1

FUNADE
C
Cut 4

FUNADE
F
Cut 6
(Reverse for 3)

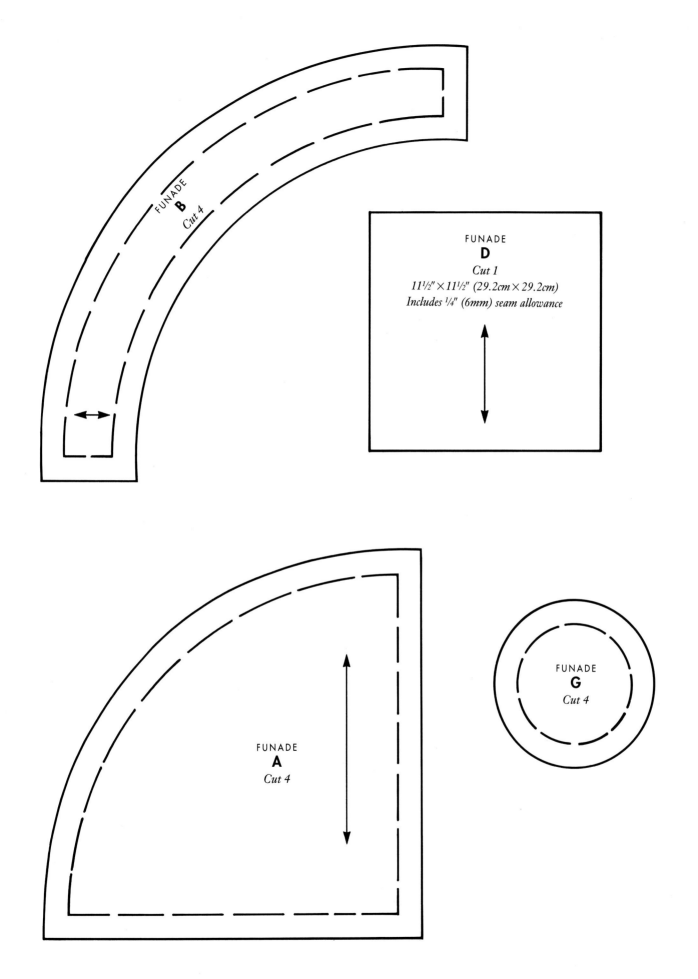

FUNADE
B
Cut 4

FUNADE
D
Cut 1
11½″ × 11½″ (29.2cm × 29.2cm)
Includes ¼″ (6mm) seam allowance

FUNADE
A
Cut 4

FUNADE
G
Cut 4

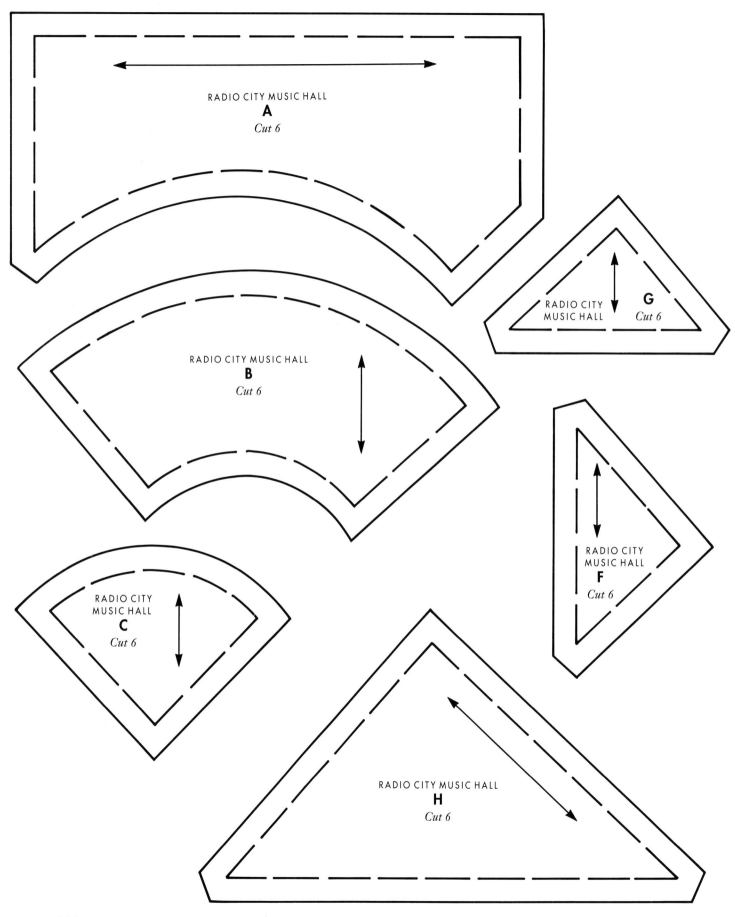

RADIO CITY MUSIC HALL
A
Cut 6

RADIO CITY MUSIC HALL
B
Cut 6

RADIO CITY
MUSIC HALL **G**
Cut 6

RADIO CITY
MUSIC HALL
C
Cut 6

RADIO CITY
MUSIC HALL
F
Cut 6

RADIO CITY MUSIC HALL
H
Cut 6

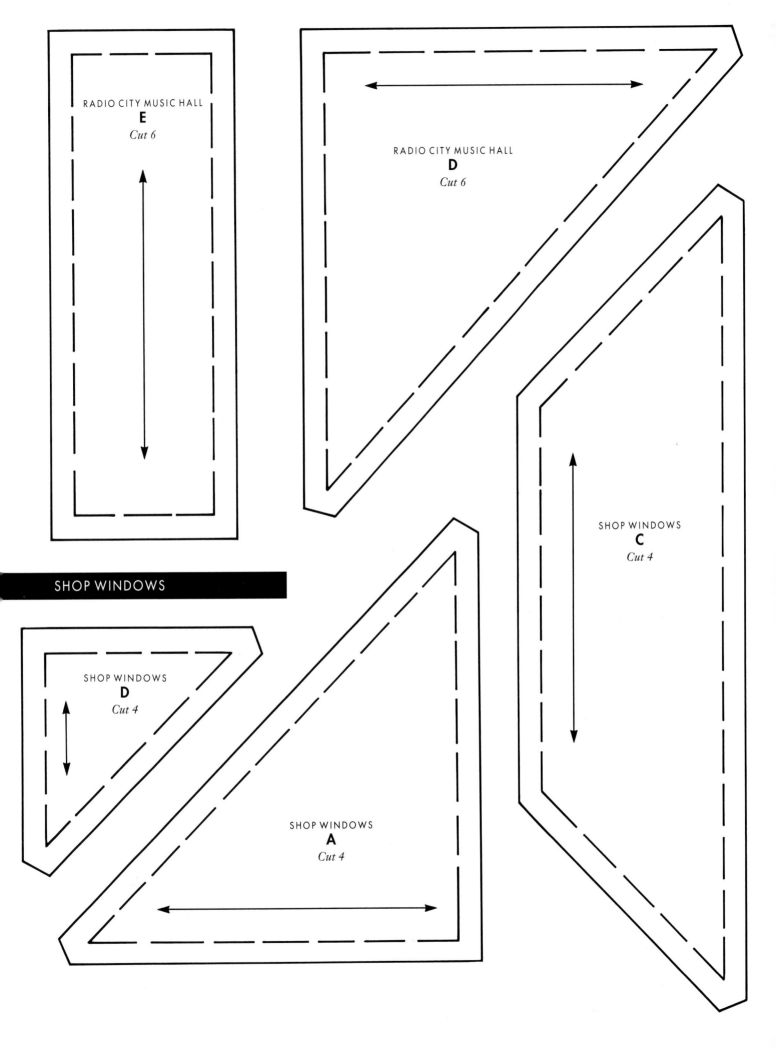

RADIO CITY MUSIC HALL
E
Cut 6

RADIO CITY MUSIC HALL
D
Cut 6

SHOP WINDOWS

SHOP WINDOWS
C
Cut 4

SHOP WINDOWS
D
Cut 4

SHOP WINDOWS
A
Cut 4

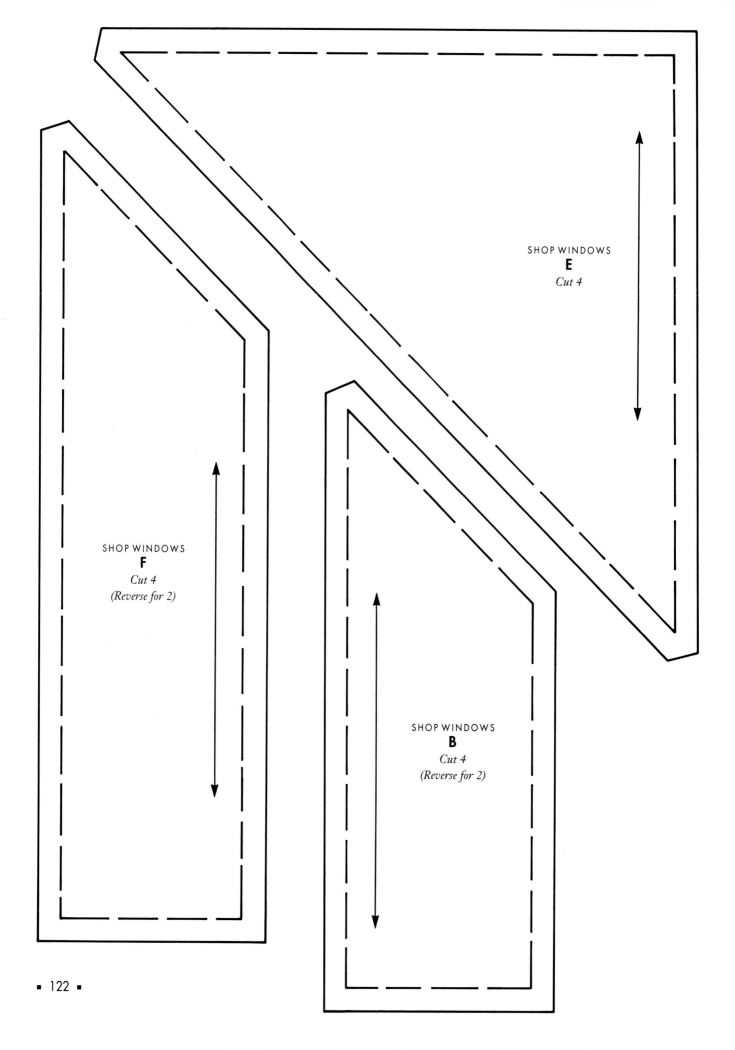

SHOP WINDOWS
E
Cut 4

SHOP WINDOWS
F
Cut 4
(Reverse for 2)

SHOP WINDOWS
B
Cut 4
(Reverse for 2)

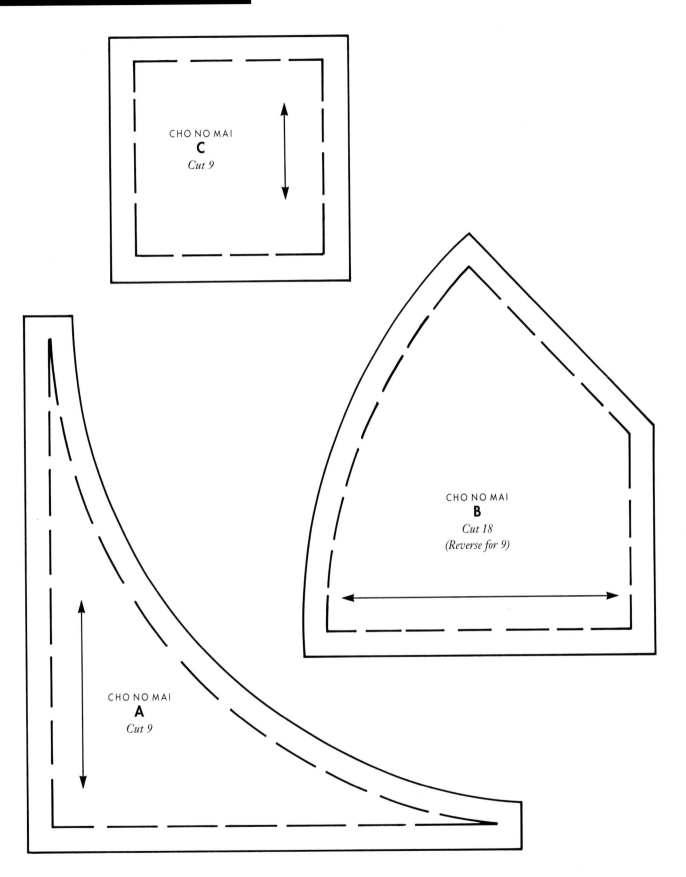

CHO NO MAI
C
Cut 9

CHO NO MAI
B
Cut 18
(Reverse for 9)

CHO NO MAI
A
Cut 9

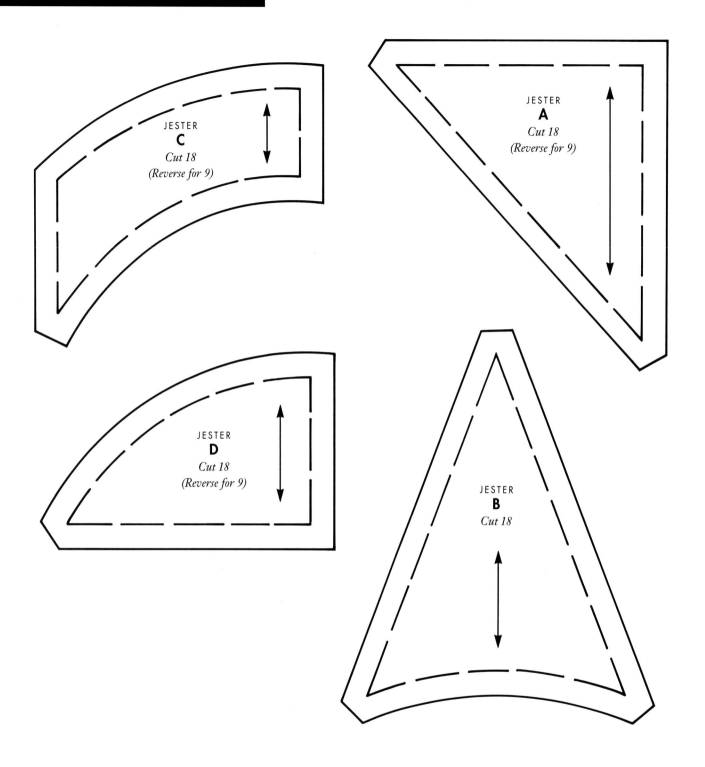

JESTER
C
Cut 18
(Reverse for 9)

JESTER
A
Cut 18
(Reverse for 9)

JESTER
D
Cut 18
(Reverse for 9)

JESTER
B
Cut 18

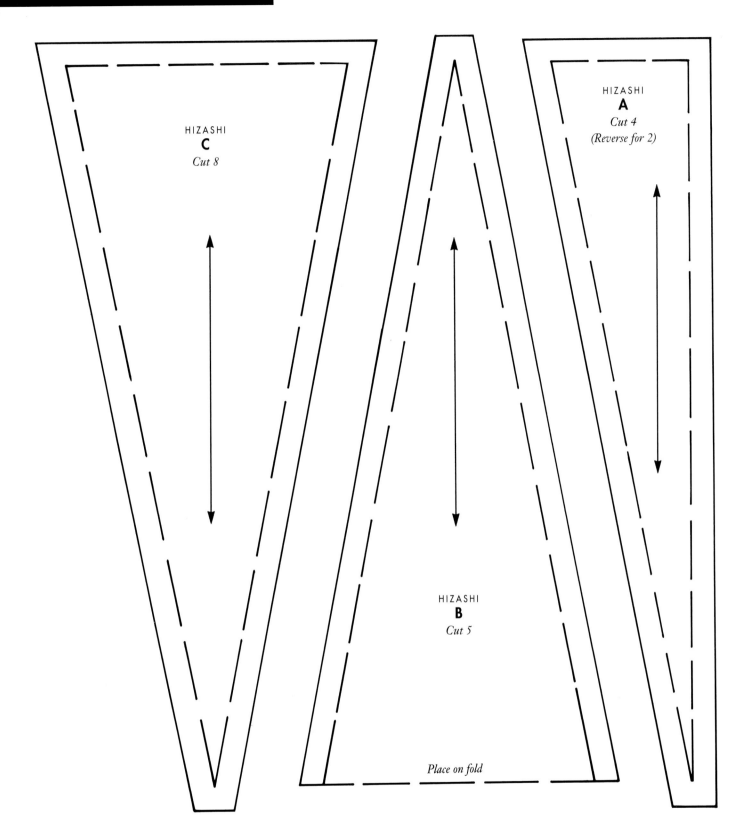

HIZASHI
C
Cut 8

HIZASHI
A
Cut 4
(Reverse for 2)

HIZASHI
B
Cut 5

Place on fold

*Note: The templates indicate the number of pieces needed for making **one block**. To determine the number of pieces needed to make a complete quilt, refer to the cutting charts that accompany the quilt instructions.*

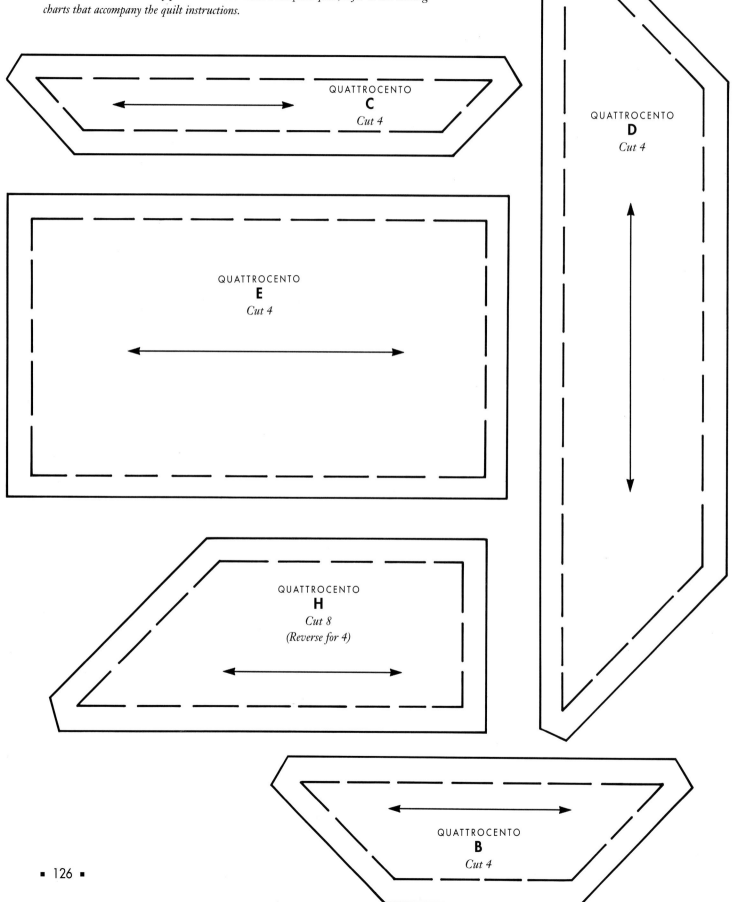

QUATTROCENTO
C
Cut 4

QUATTROCENTO
D
Cut 4

QUATTROCENTO
E
Cut 4

QUATTROCENTO
H
Cut 8
(Reverse for 4)

QUATTROCENTO
B
Cut 4

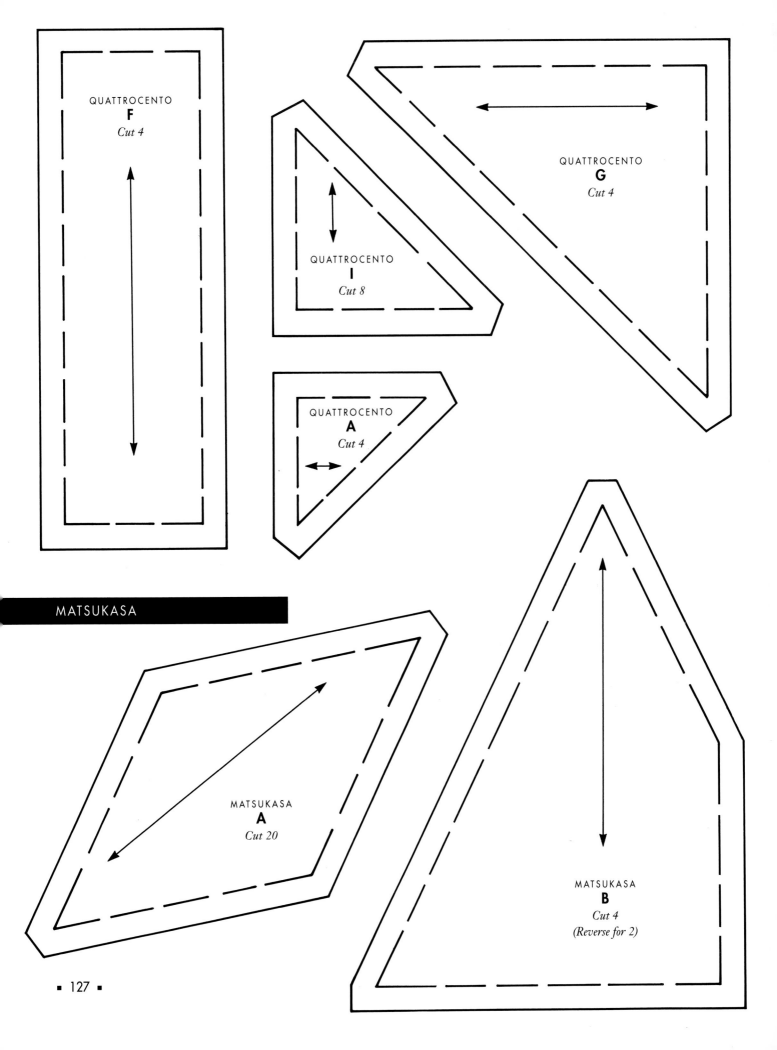

QUATTROCENTO
F
Cut 4

QUATTROCENTO
I
Cut 8

QUATTROCENTO
G
Cut 4

QUATTROCENTO
A
Cut 4

MATSUKASA

MATSUKASA
A
Cut 20

MATSUKASA
B
Cut 4
(Reverse for 2)

■ 127 ■

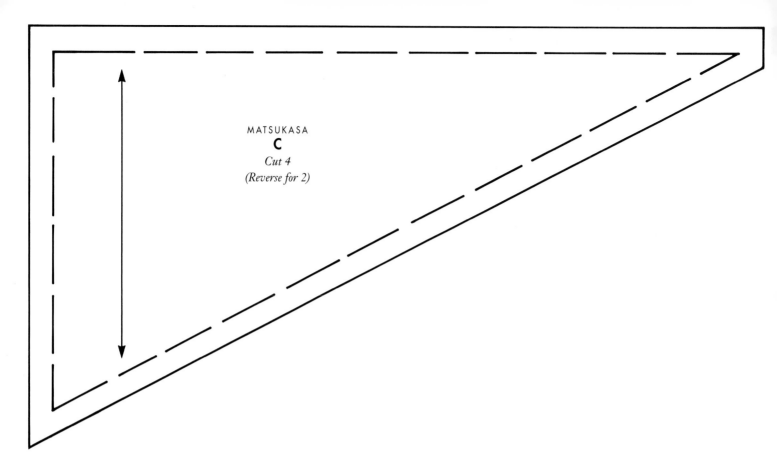

MATSUKASA
C
Cut 4
(Reverse for 2)

KANZASHI

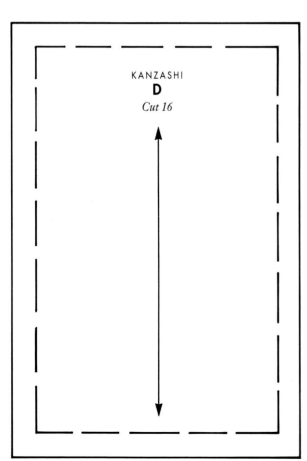

KANZASHI
D
Cut 16

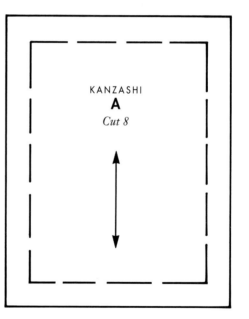

KANZASHI
A
Cut 8

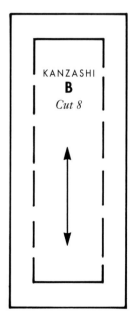

KANZASHI
B
Cut 8

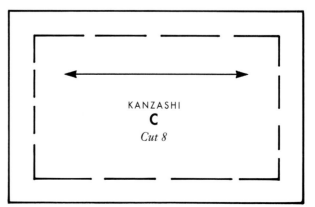

KANZASHI
C
Cut 8

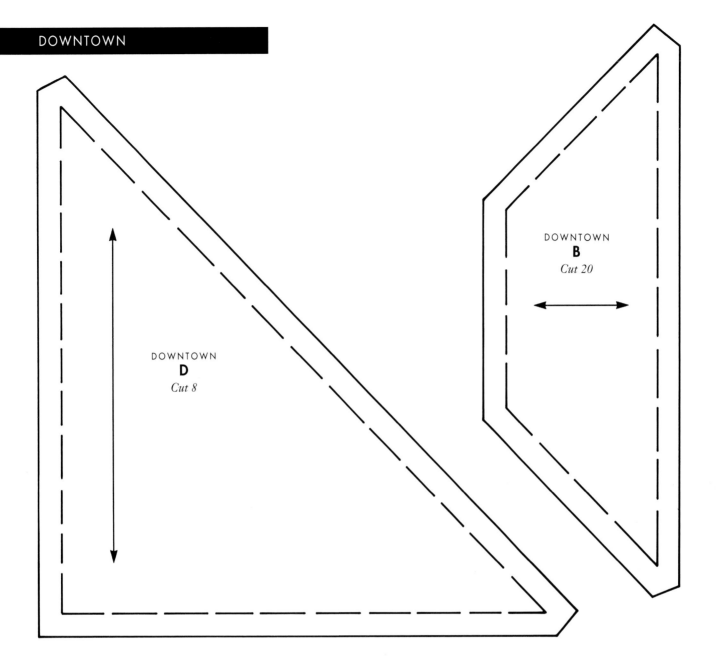

DOWNTOWN
B
Cut 20

DOWNTOWN
D
Cut 8

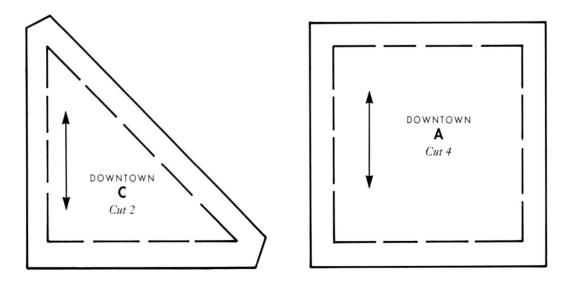

DOWNTOWN
C
Cut 2

DOWNTOWN
A
Cut 4

FUYUDORI

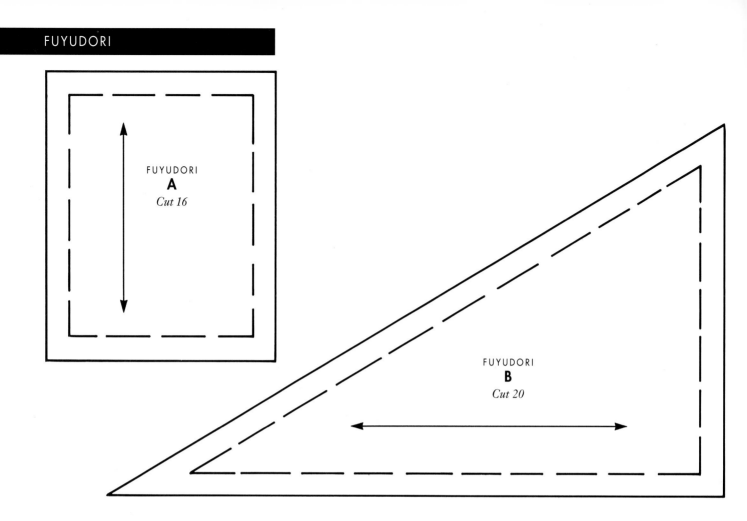

FUYUDORI
A
Cut 16

FUYUDORI
B
Cut 20

MORNING GLORY

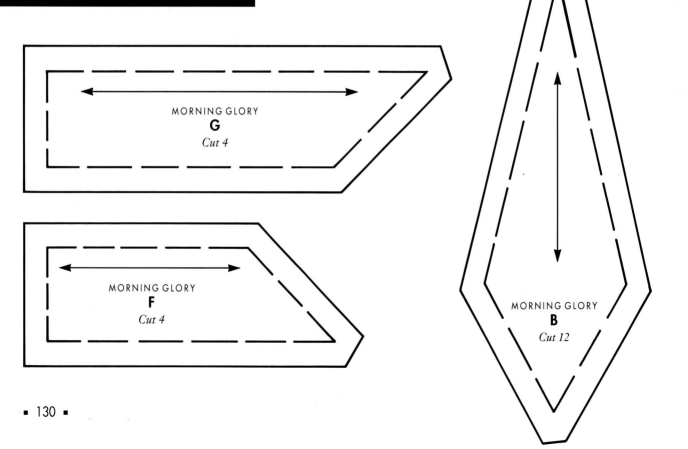

MORNING GLORY
G
Cut 4

MORNING GLORY
F
Cut 4

MORNING GLORY
B
Cut 12

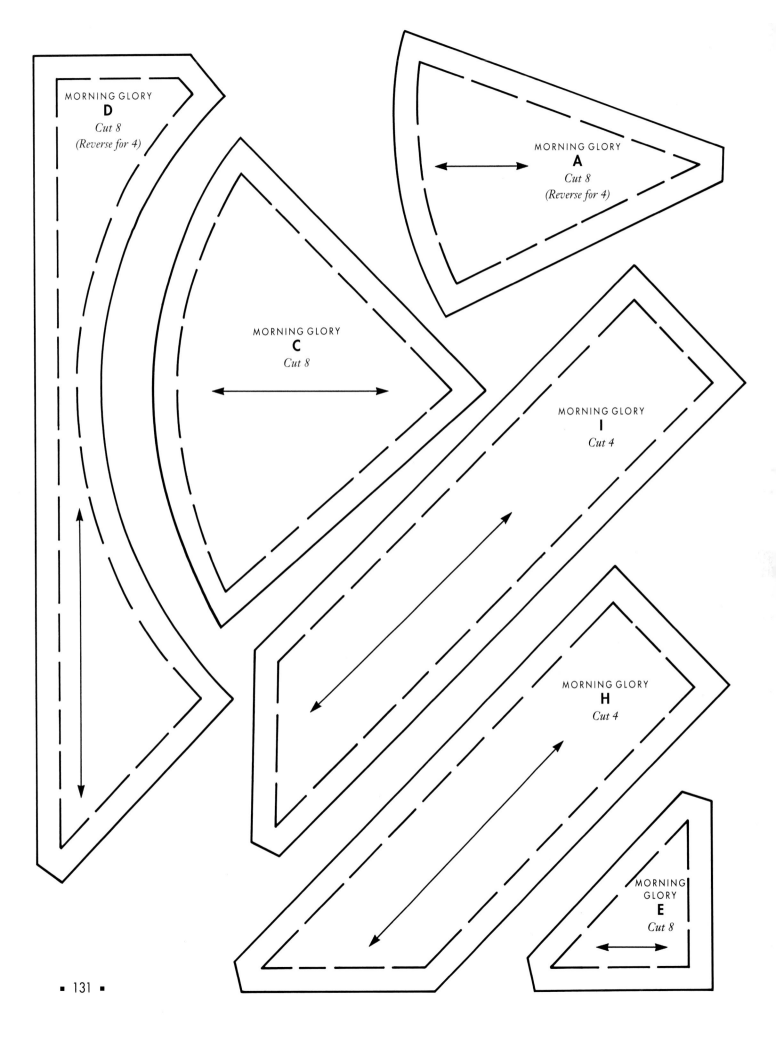

MORNING GLORY
D
Cut 8
(Reverse for 4)

MORNING GLORY
A
Cut 8
(Reverse for 4)

MORNING GLORY
C
Cut 8

MORNING GLORY
I
Cut 4

MORNING GLORY
H
Cut 4

MORNING
GLORY
E
Cut 8

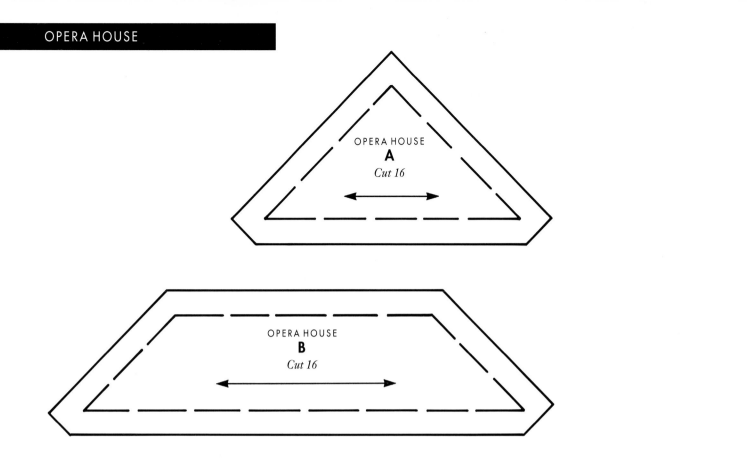

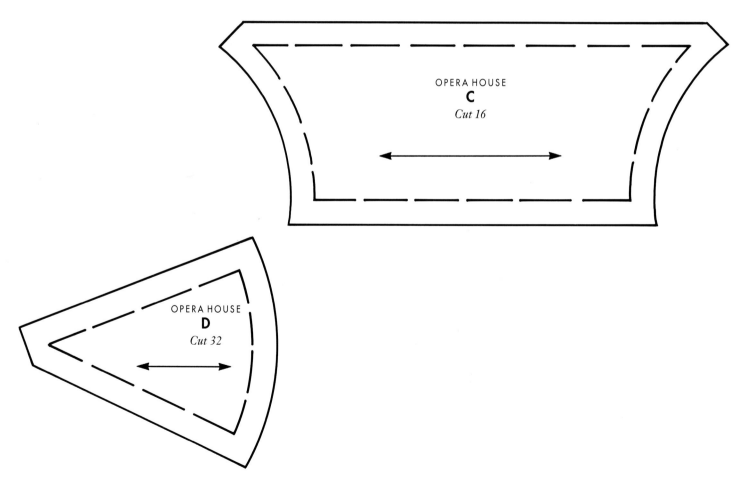

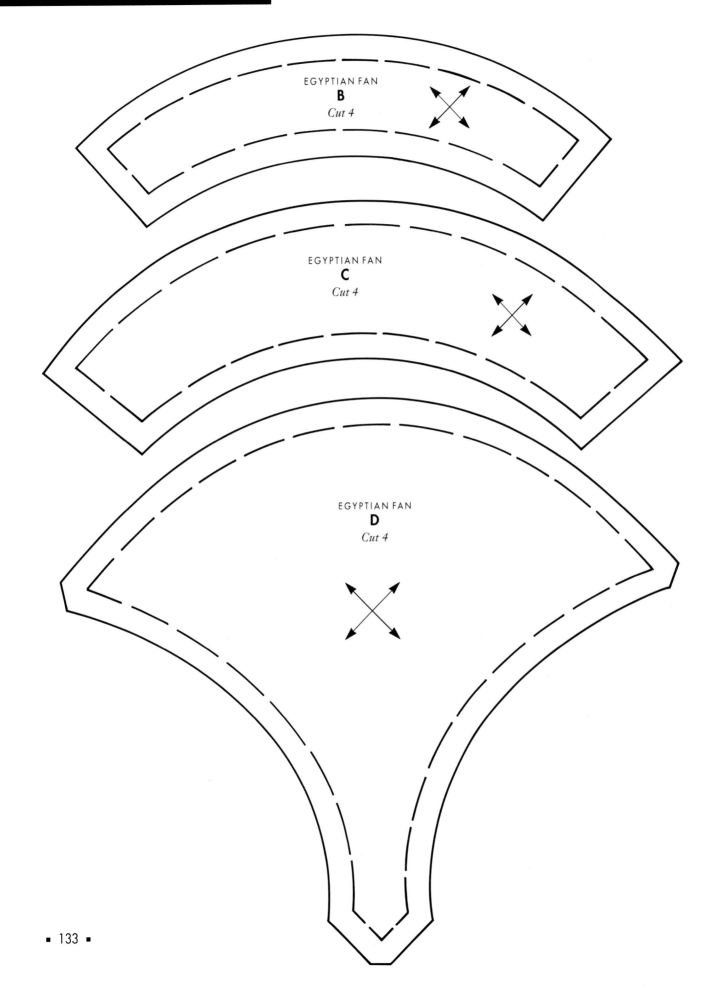

EGYPTIAN FAN
B
Cut 4

EGYPTIAN FAN
C
Cut 4

EGYPTIAN FAN
D
Cut 4

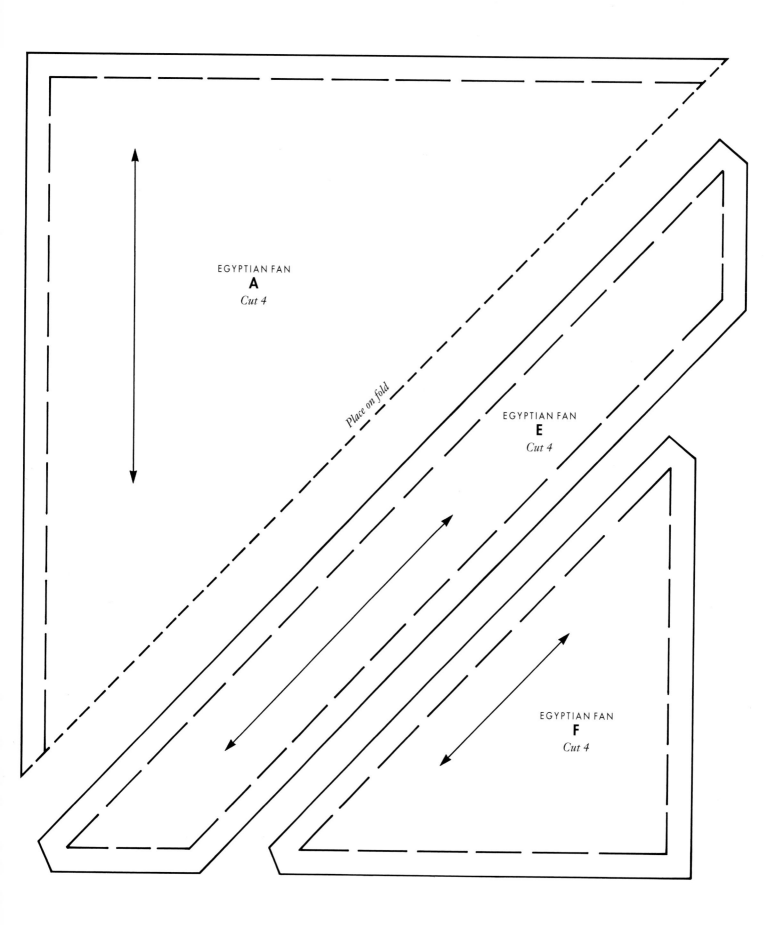

EGYPTIAN FAN
A
Cut 4

Place on fold

EGYPTIAN FAN
E
Cut 4

EGYPTIAN FAN
F
Cut 4

NOTE: *The templates indicate the number of pieces needed for making* **one block.** *To determine the number of pieces needed to make a complete quilt, refer to the cutting charts that accompany the quilt instructions.*

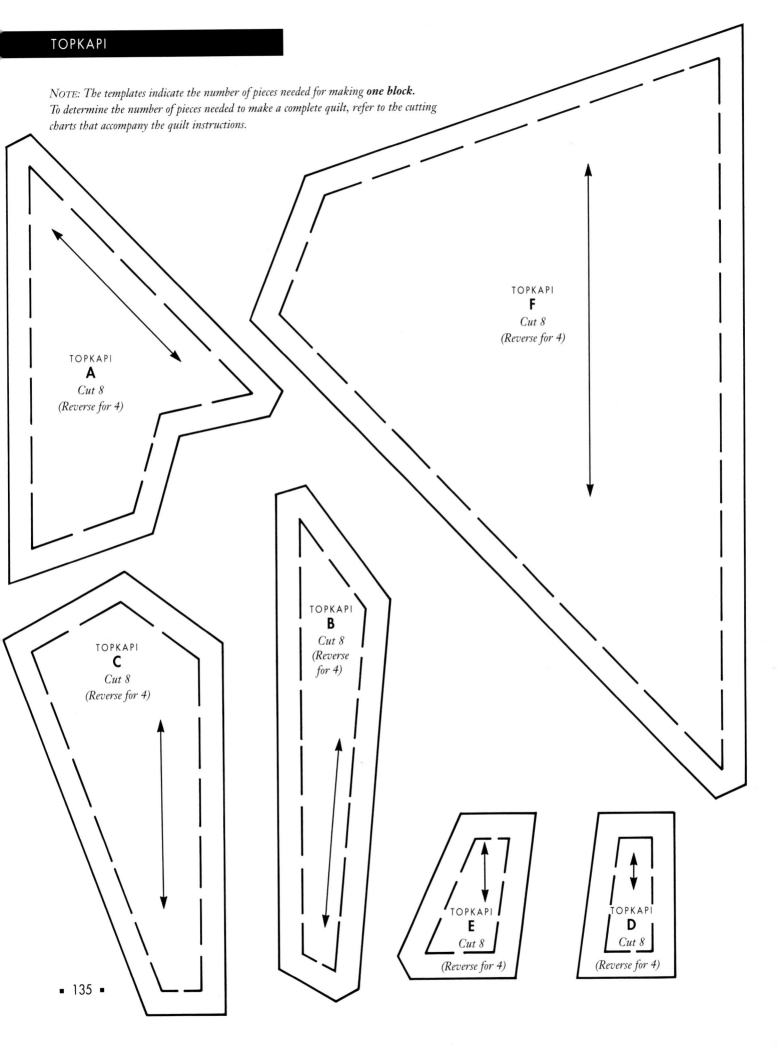

TOPKAPI
A
Cut 8
(Reverse for 4)

TOPKAPI
F
Cut 8
(Reverse for 4)

TOPKAPI
C
Cut 8
(Reverse for 4)

TOPKAPI
B
Cut 8
(Reverse for 4)

TOPKAPI
E
Cut 8
(Reverse for 4)

TOPKAPI
D
Cut 8
(Reverse for 4)

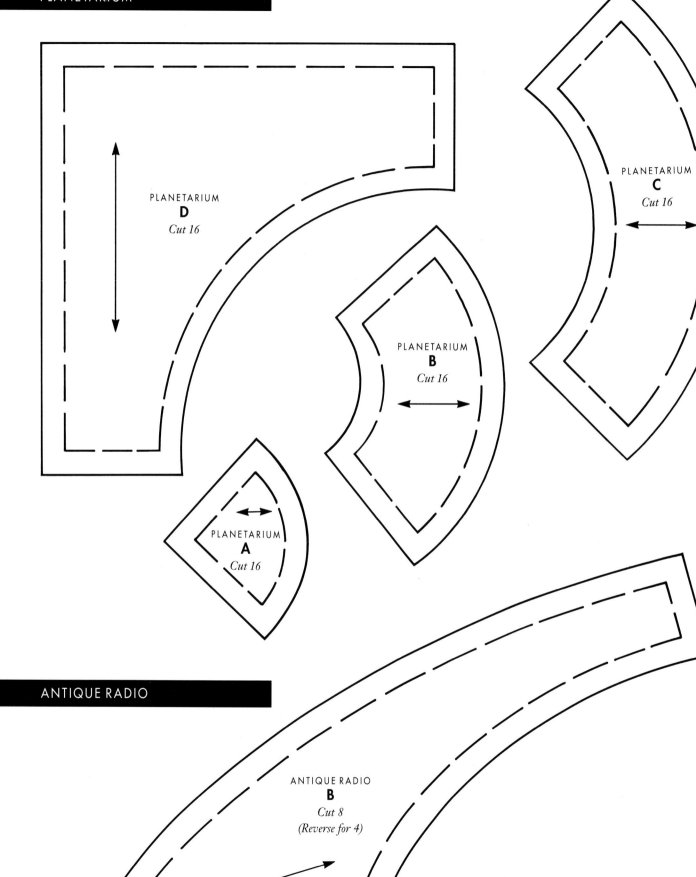

PLANETARIUM

PLANETARIUM
D
Cut 16

PLANETARIUM
C
Cut 16

PLANETARIUM
B
Cut 16

PLANETARIUM
A
Cut 16

ANTIQUE RADIO

ANTIQUE RADIO
B
Cut 8
(Reverse for 4)

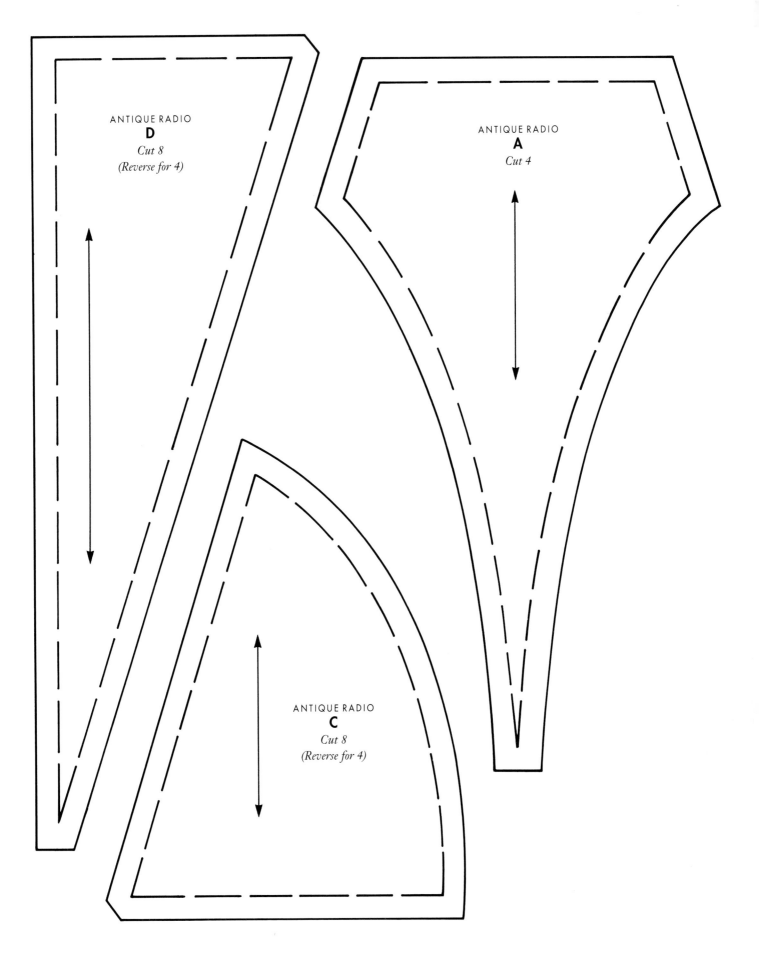

ANTIQUE RADIO
D
Cut 8
(Reverse for 4)

ANTIQUE RADIO
A
Cut 4

ANTIQUE RADIO
C
Cut 8
(Reverse for 4)

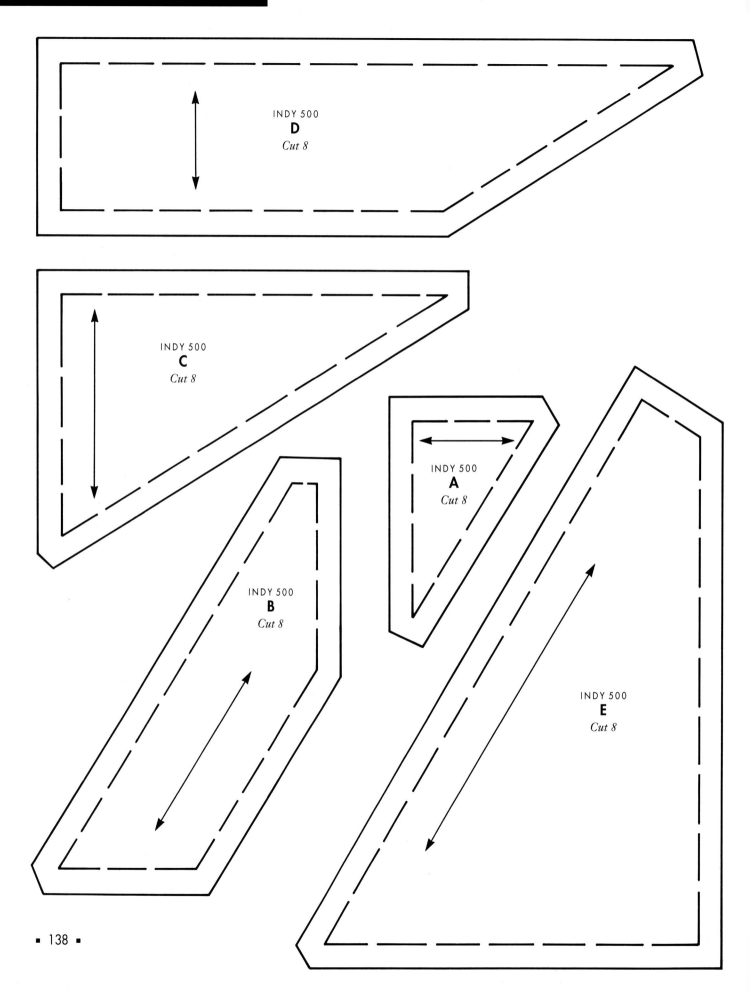

INDY 500
D
Cut 8

INDY 500
C
Cut 8

INDY 500
A
Cut 8

INDY 500
B
Cut 8

INDY 500
E
Cut 8

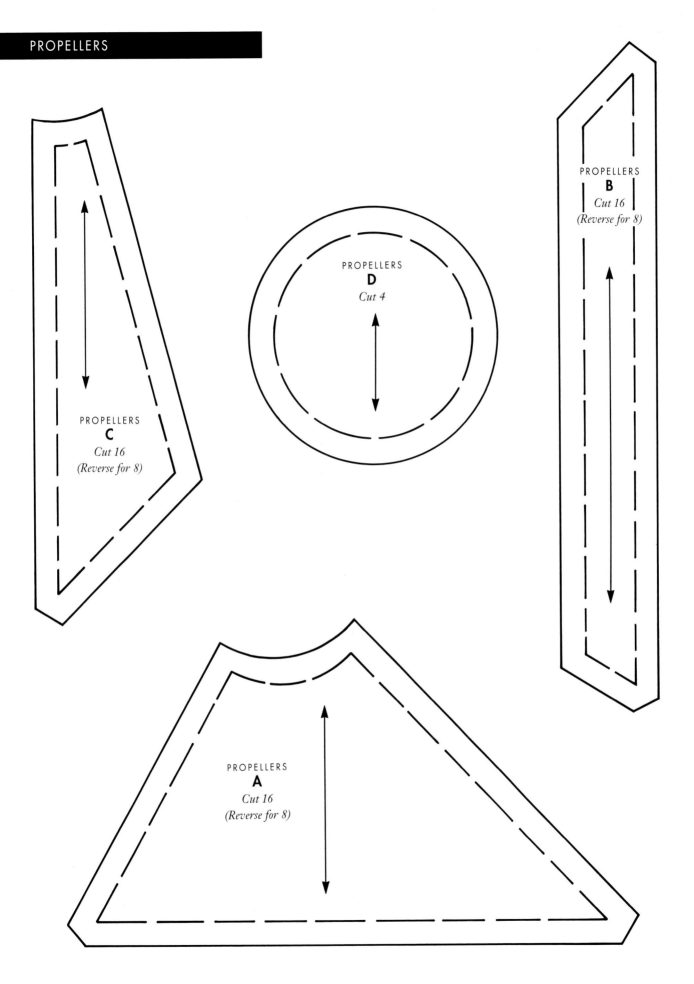

PROPELLERS
B
Cut 16
(Reverse for 8)

PROPELLERS
D
Cut 4

PROPELLERS
C
Cut 16
(Reverse for 8)

PROPELLERS
A
Cut 16
(Reverse for 8)

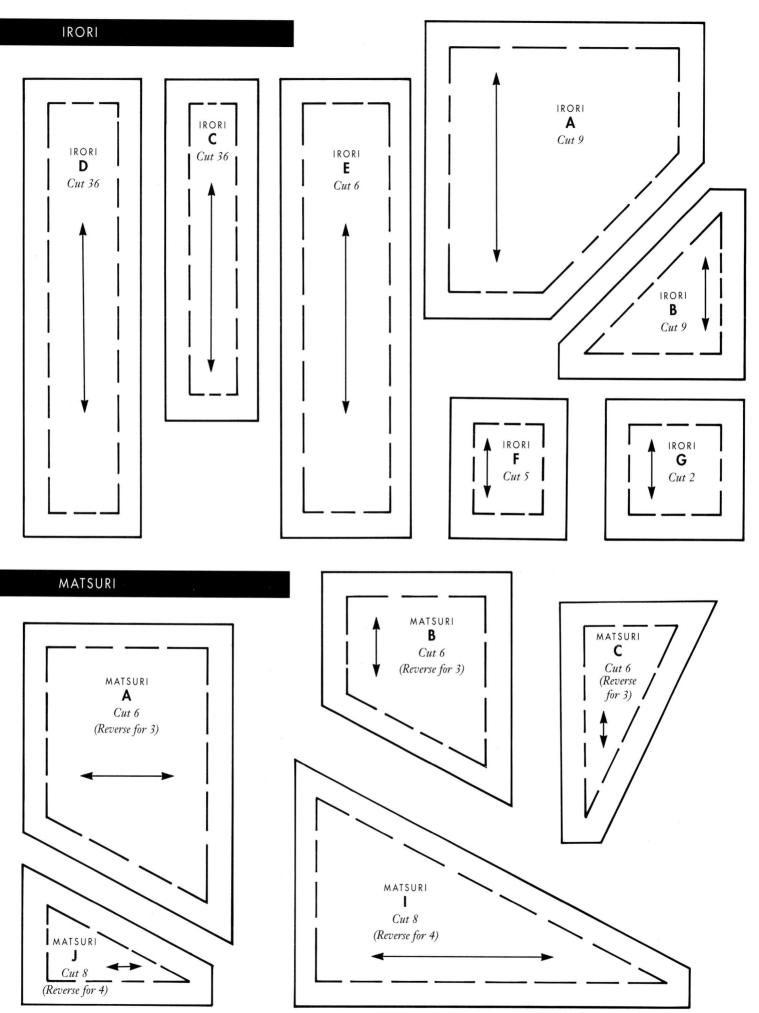

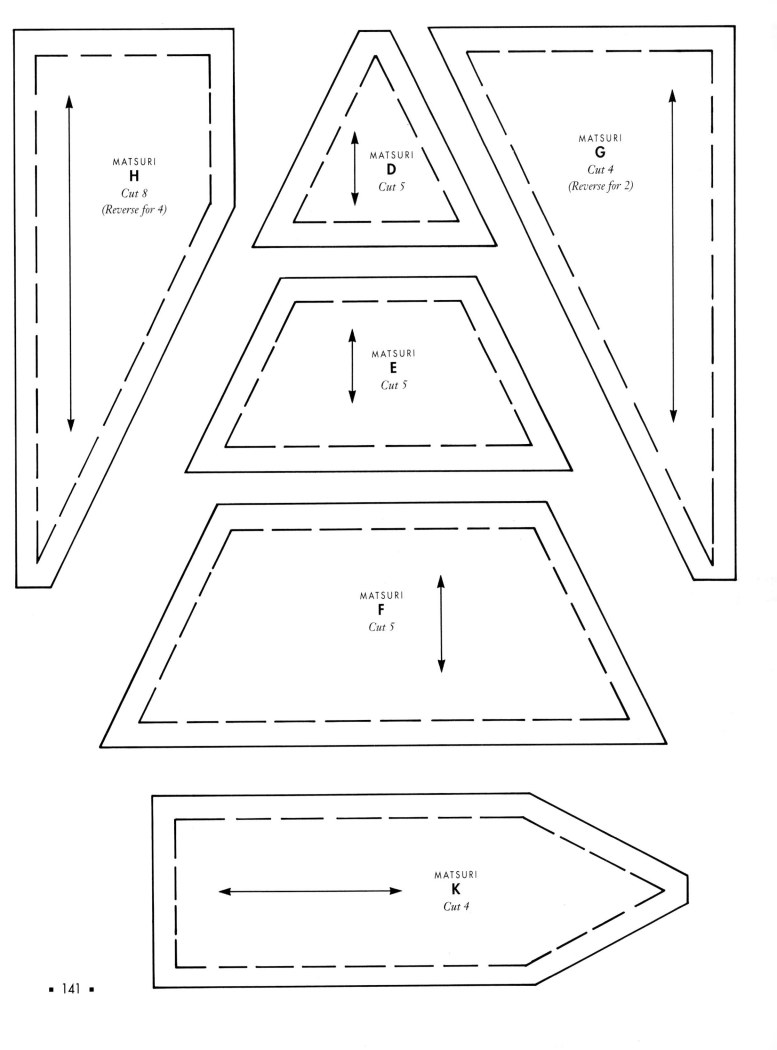

MATSURI
H
Cut 8
(Reverse for 4)

MATSURI
D
Cut 5

MATSURI
G
Cut 4
(Reverse for 2)

MATSURI
E
Cut 5

MATSURI
F
Cut 5

MATSURI
K
Cut 4

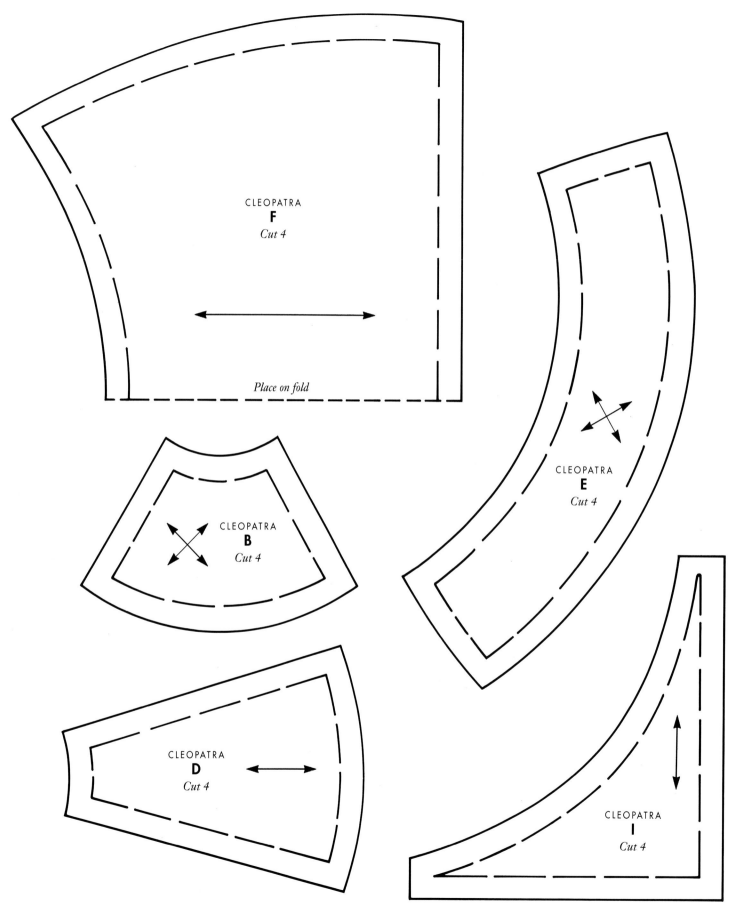

CLEOPATRA
F
Cut 4

Place on fold

CLEOPATRA
E
Cut 4

CLEOPATRA
B
Cut 4

CLEOPATRA
D
Cut 4

CLEOPATRA
I
Cut 4

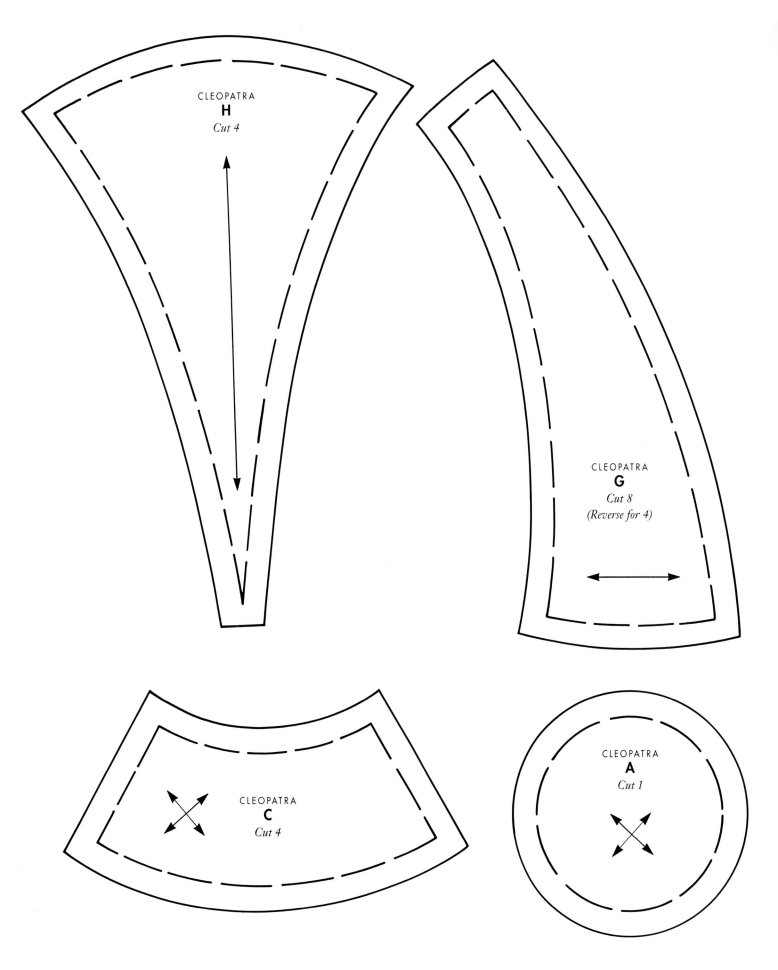

CLEOPATRA
H
Cut 4

CLEOPATRA
G
Cut 8
(Reverse for 4)

CLEOPATRA
C
Cut 4

CLEOPATRA
A
Cut 1

NOTE: *The templates indicate the number of pieces needed for making* **one block.**
To determine the number of pieces needed to make a complete quilt, refer to the cutting charts that accompany the quilt instructions.

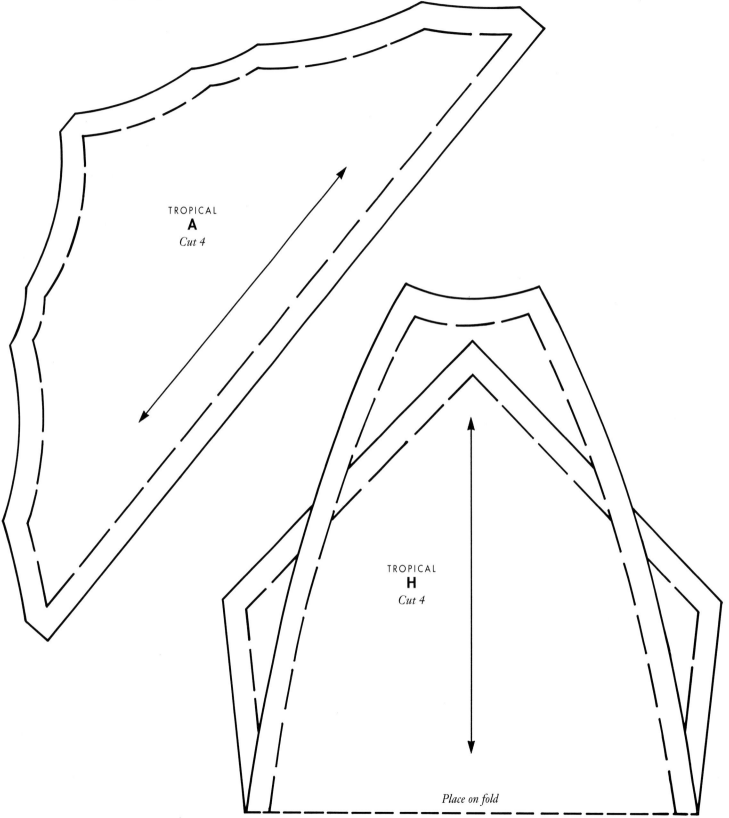

TROPICAL
A
Cut 4

TROPICAL
H
Cut 4

Place on fold

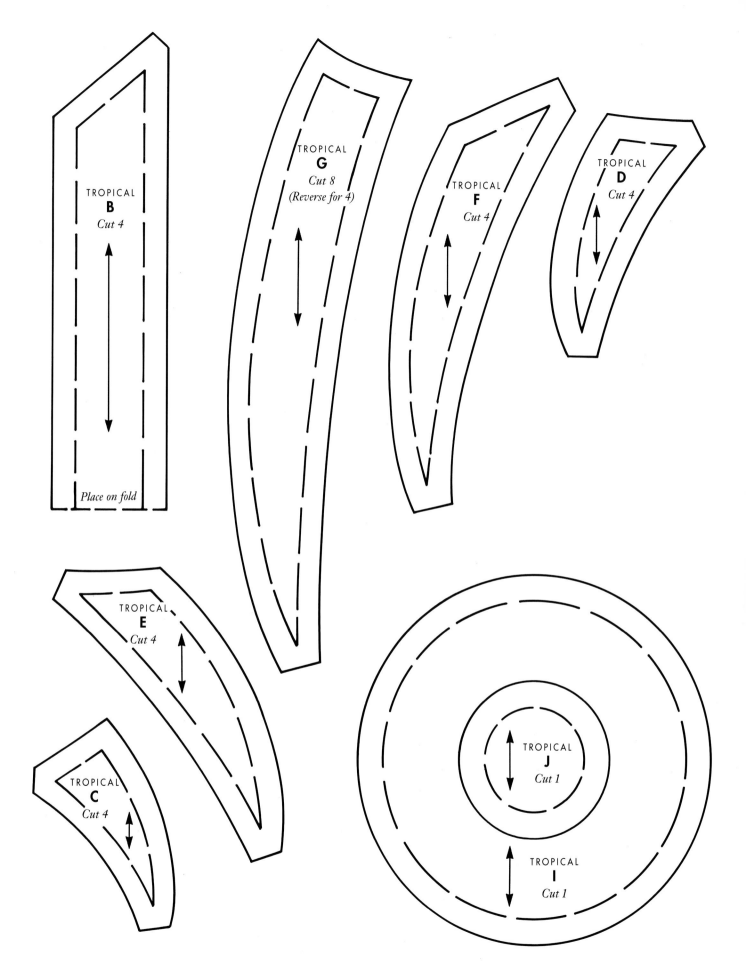

TROPICAL
B
Cut 4

Place on fold

TROPICAL
G
Cut 8
(Reverse for 4)

TROPICAL
F
Cut 4

TROPICAL
D
Cut 4

TROPICAL
E
Cut 4

TROPICAL
C
Cut 4

TROPICAL
J
Cut 1

TROPICAL
I
Cut 1

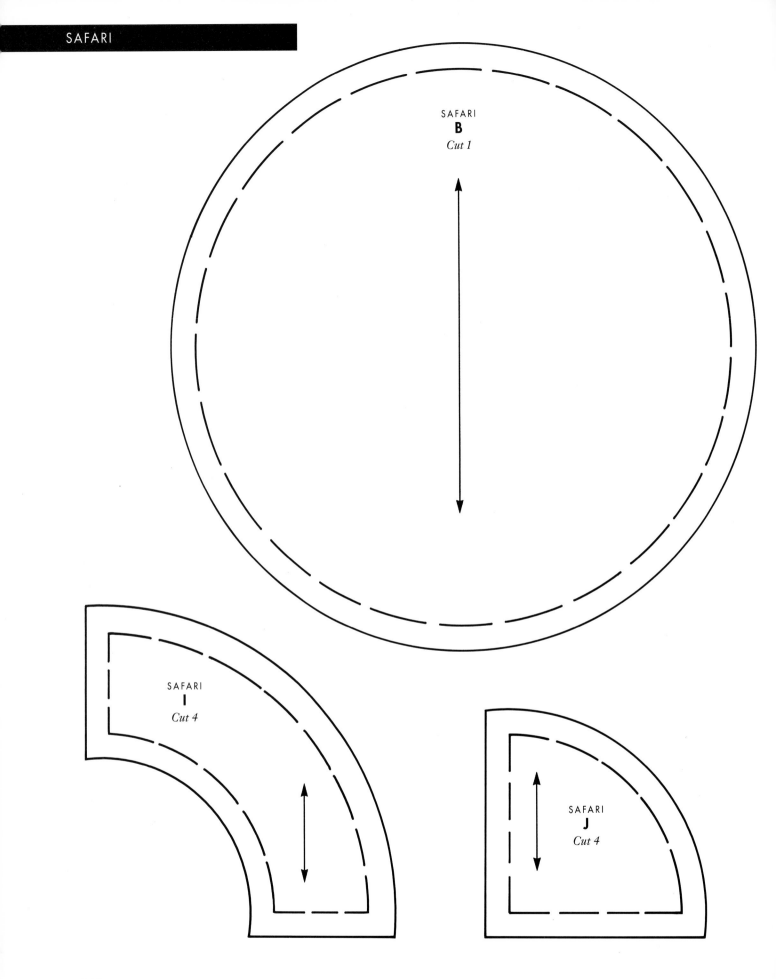

SAFARI
B
Cut 1

SAFARI
I
Cut 4

SAFARI
J
Cut 4

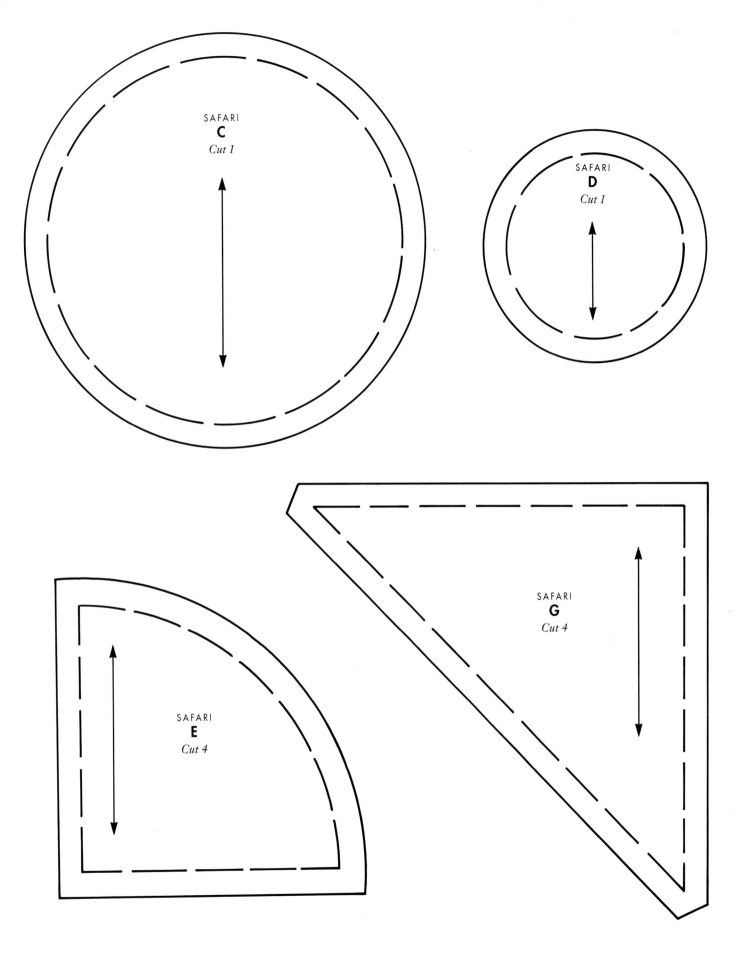

SAFARI
C
Cut 1

SAFARI
D
Cut 1

SAFARI
G
Cut 4

SAFARI
E
Cut 4

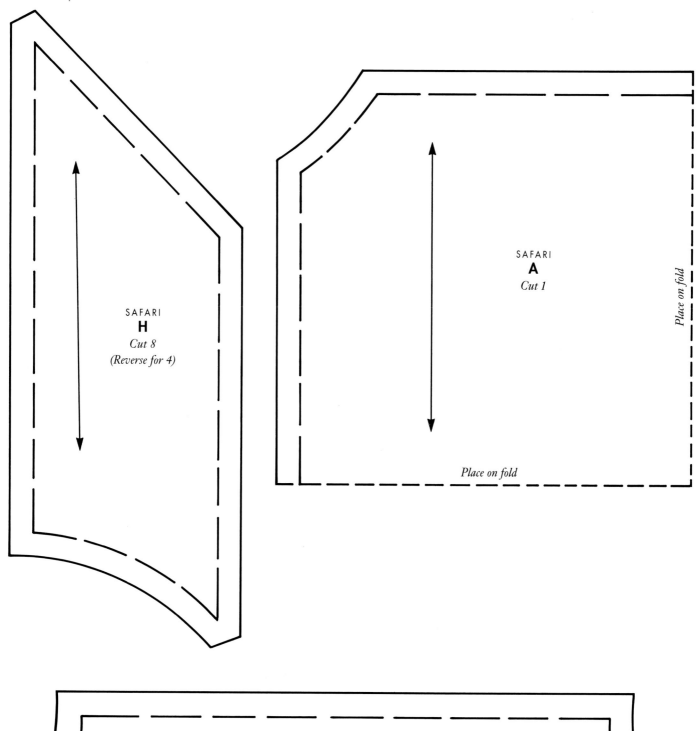

SAFARI
H
Cut 8
(Reverse for 4)

SAFARI
A
Cut 1

Place on fold

Place on fold

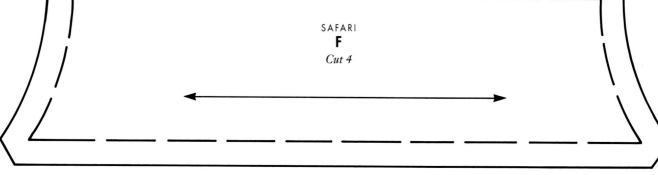

SAFARI
F
Cut 4

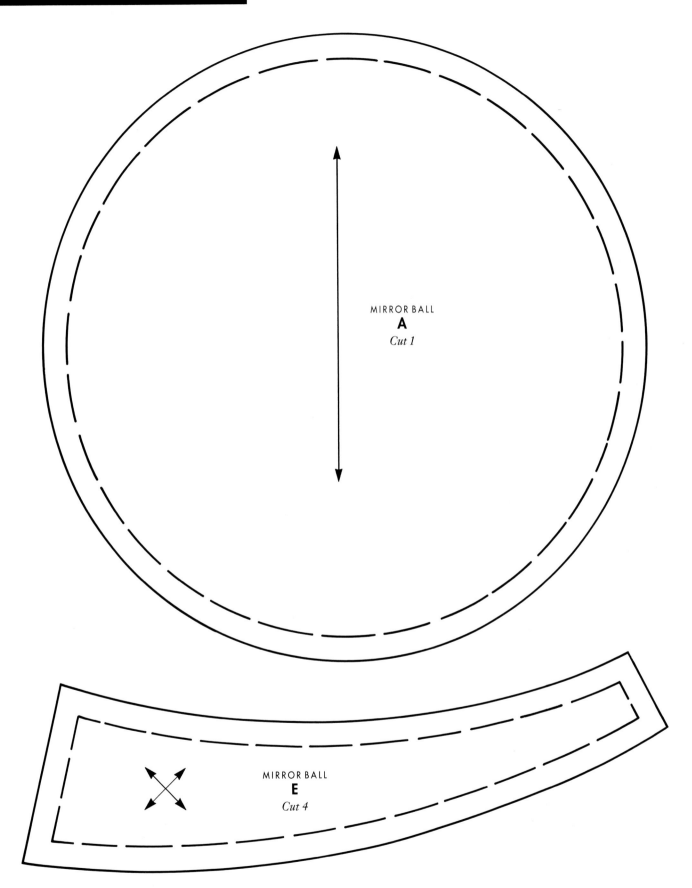

MIRROR BALL
A
Cut 1

MIRROR BALL
E
Cut 4

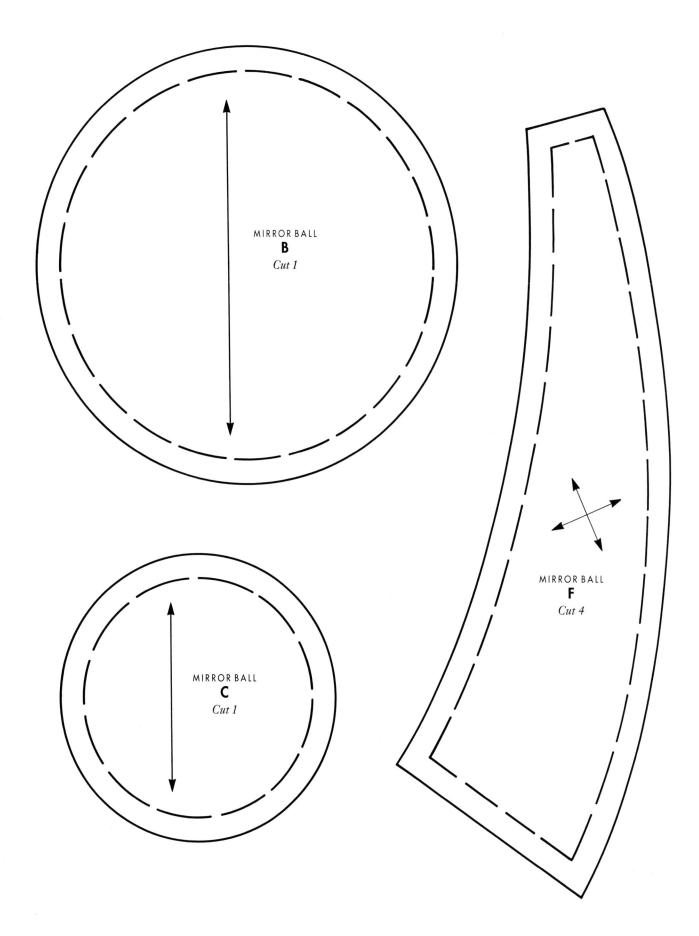

MIRROR BALL
B
Cut 1

MIRROR BALL
C
Cut 1

MIRROR BALL
F
Cut 4

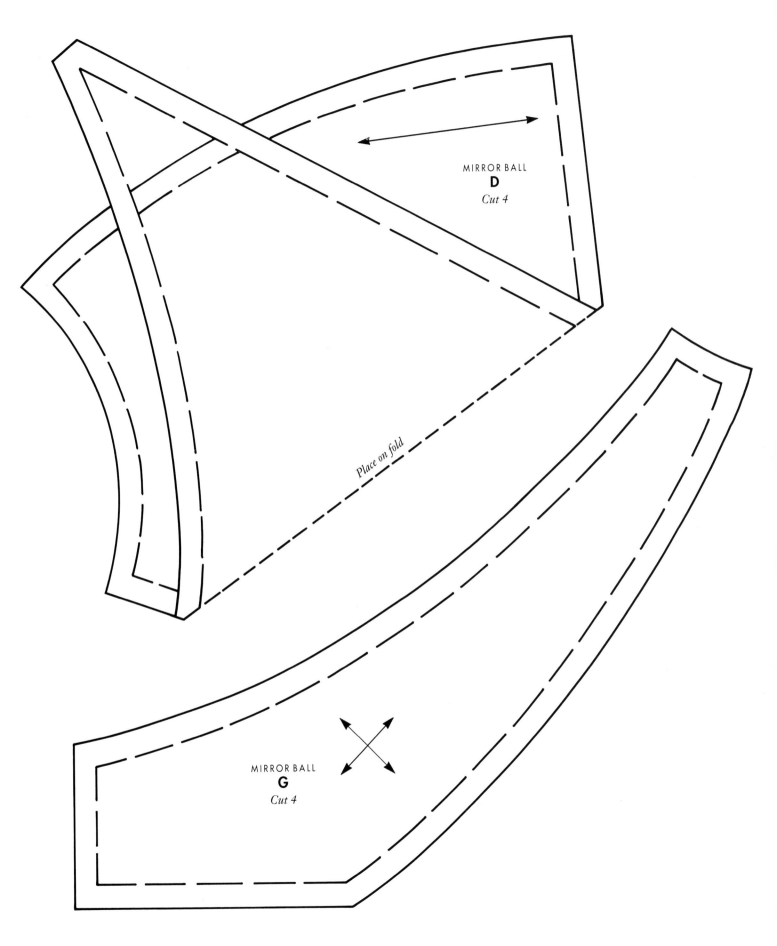

MIRROR BALL
D
Cut 4

Place on fold

MIRROR BALL
G
Cut 4

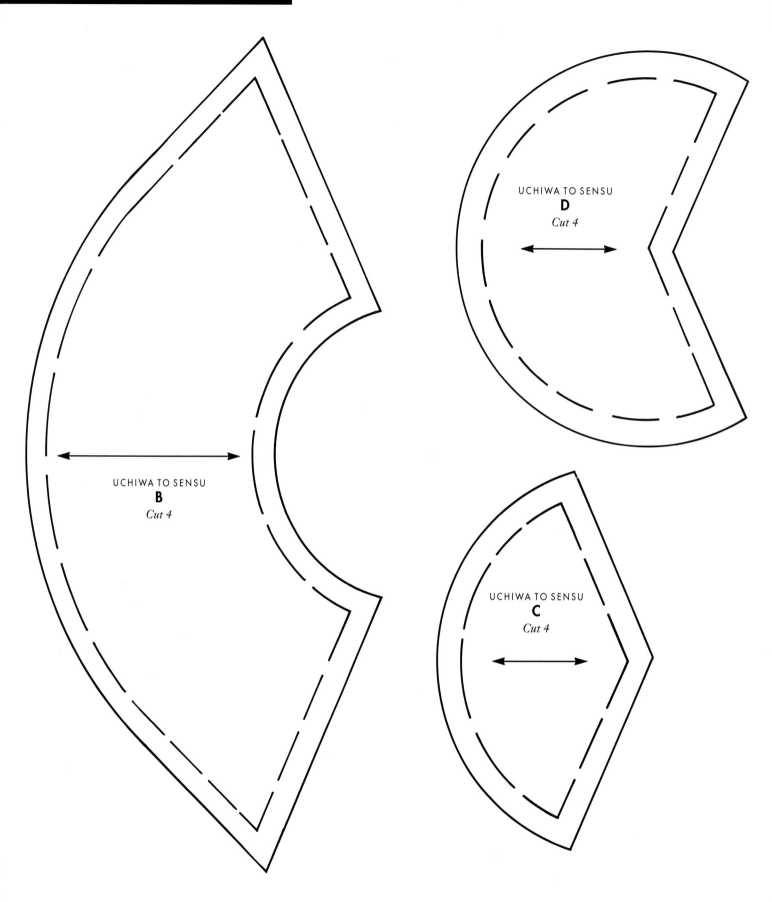

UCHIWA TO SENSU
D
Cut 4

UCHIWA TO SENSU
B
Cut 4

UCHIWA TO SENSU
C
Cut 4

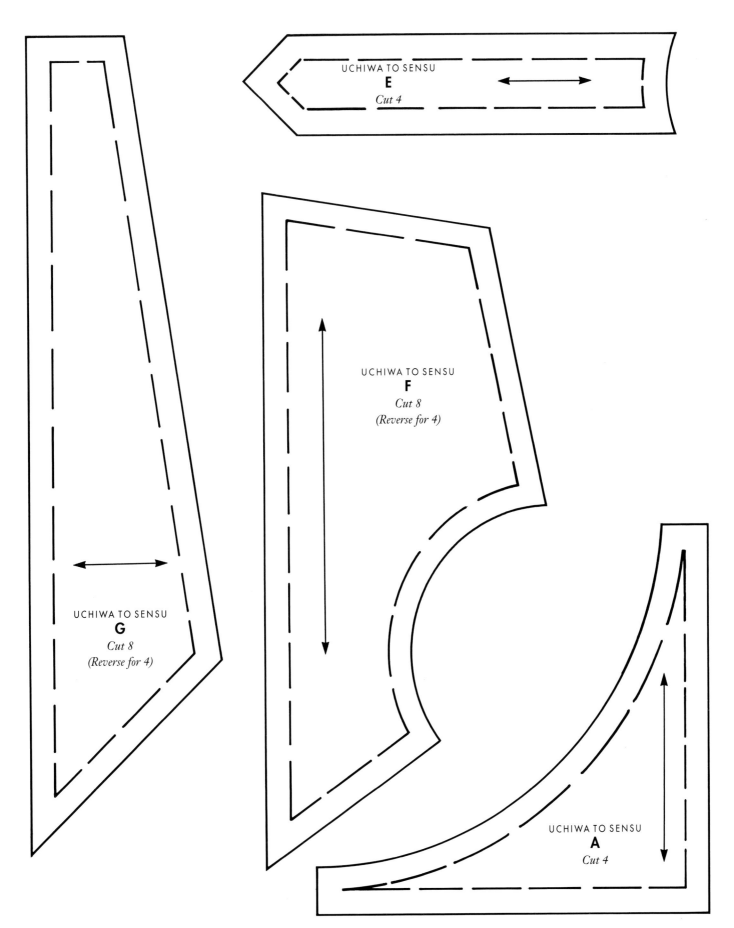

UCHIWA TO SENSU
E
Cut 4

UCHIWA TO SENSU
F
Cut 8
(Reverse for 4)

UCHIWA TO SENSU
G
Cut 8
(Reverse for 4)

UCHIWA TO SENSU
A
Cut 4

NOTE: Grain direction is optional on templates without grainlines.

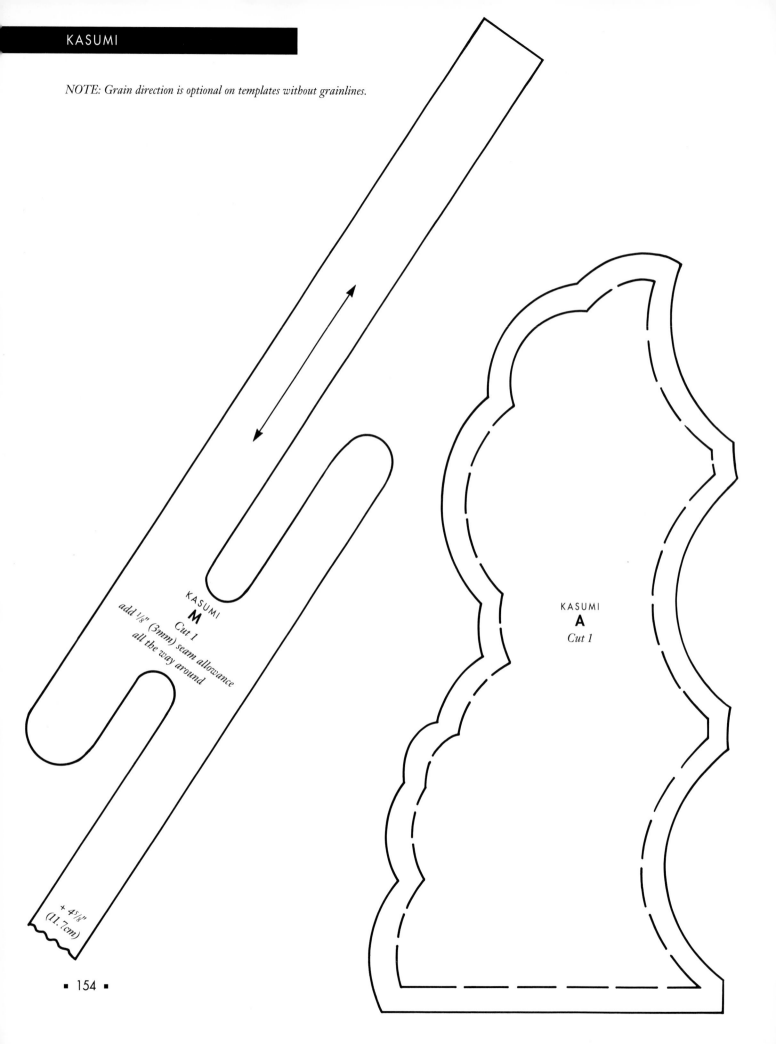

KASUMI
M
Cut 1
add ⅛" (3mm) seam allowance
all the way around

+ 4⅝"
(11.7cm)

KASUMI
A
Cut 1

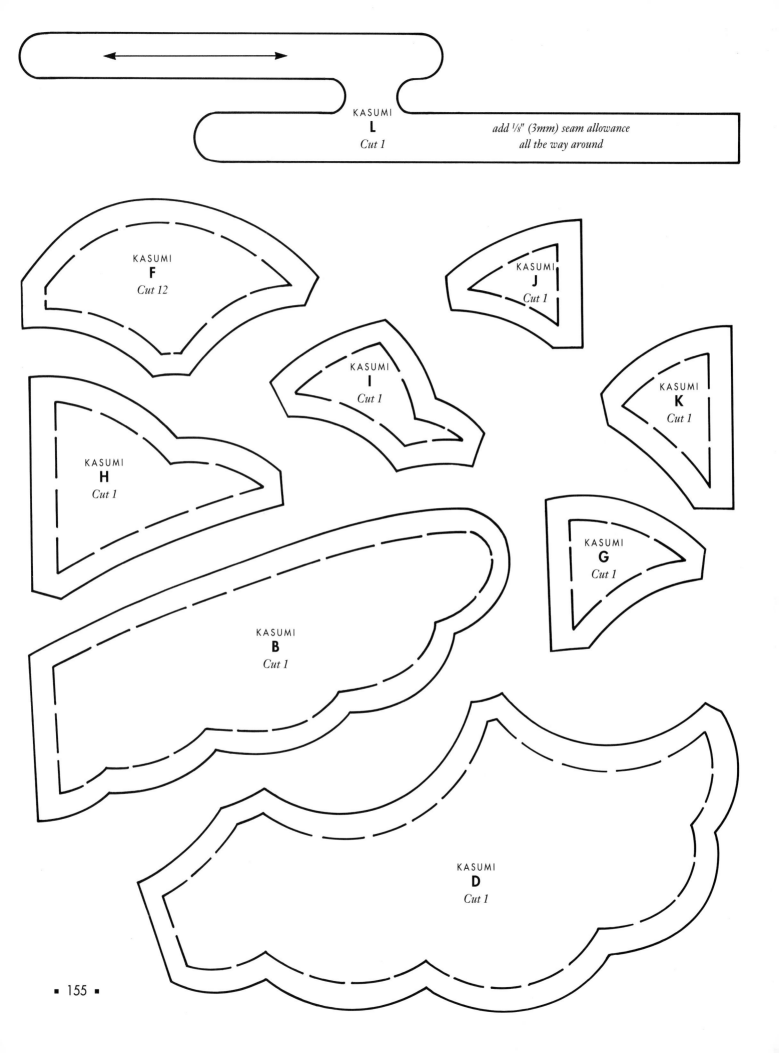

KASUMI
L
Cut 1

*add ⅛" (3mm) seam allowance
all the way around*

KASUMI
F
Cut 12

KASUMI
J
Cut 1

KASUMI
I
Cut 1

KASUMI
K
Cut 1

KASUMI
H
Cut 1

KASUMI
G
Cut 1

KASUMI
B
Cut 1

KASUMI
D
Cut 1

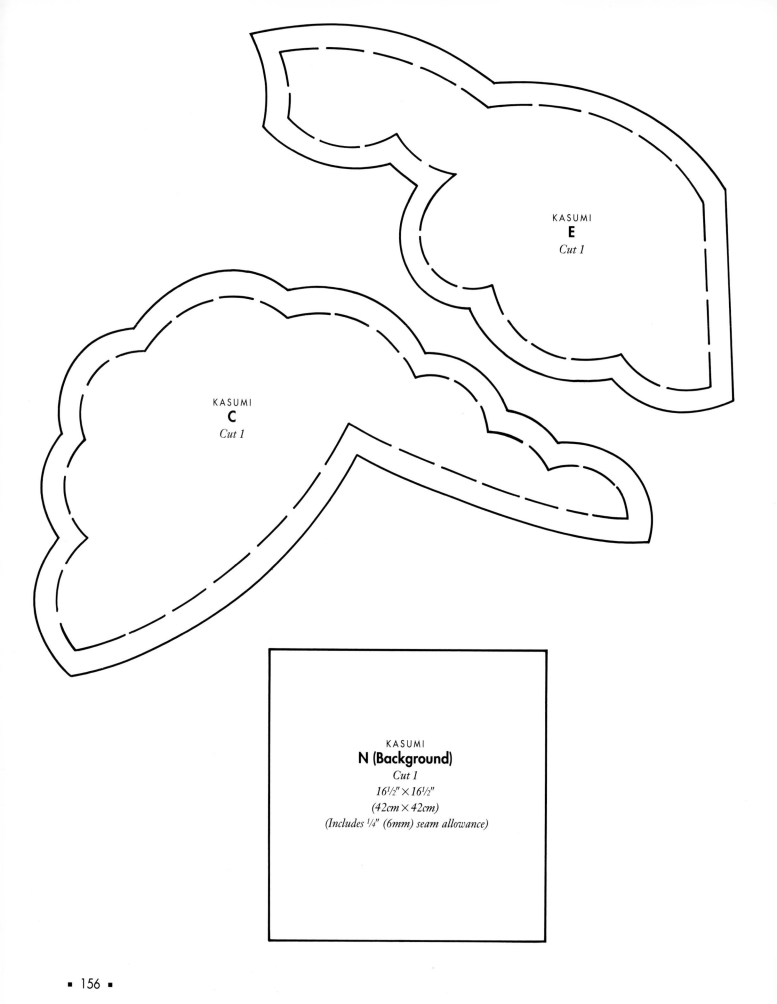

KASUMI
E
Cut 1

KASUMI
C
Cut 1

KASUMI
N (Background)
Cut 1
16¹⁄₂" × 16¹⁄₂"
(42cm × 42cm)
(Includes ¹⁄₄" (6mm) seam allowance)

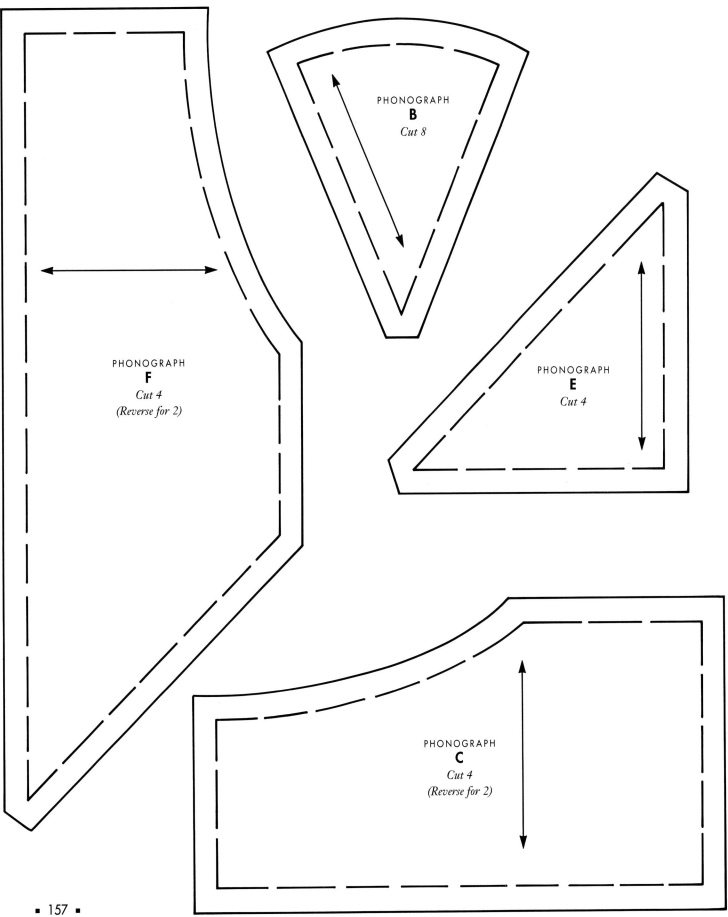

PHONOGRAPH
B
Cut 8

PHONOGRAPH
F
Cut 4
(Reverse for 2)

PHONOGRAPH
E
Cut 4

PHONOGRAPH
C
Cut 4
(Reverse for 2)

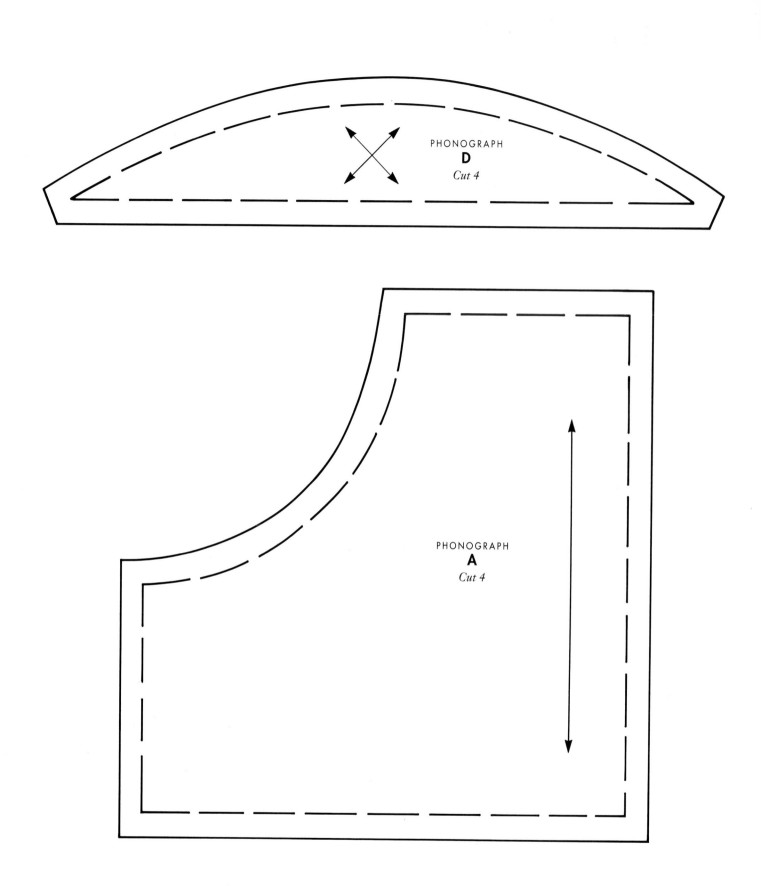

PHONOGRAPH
D
Cut 4

PHONOGRAPH
A
Cut 4

NOTE: *The templates indicate the number of pieces needed for making* **one block.** *To determine the number of pieces needed to make a complete quilt, refer to the cutting charts that accompany the quilt instructions.*

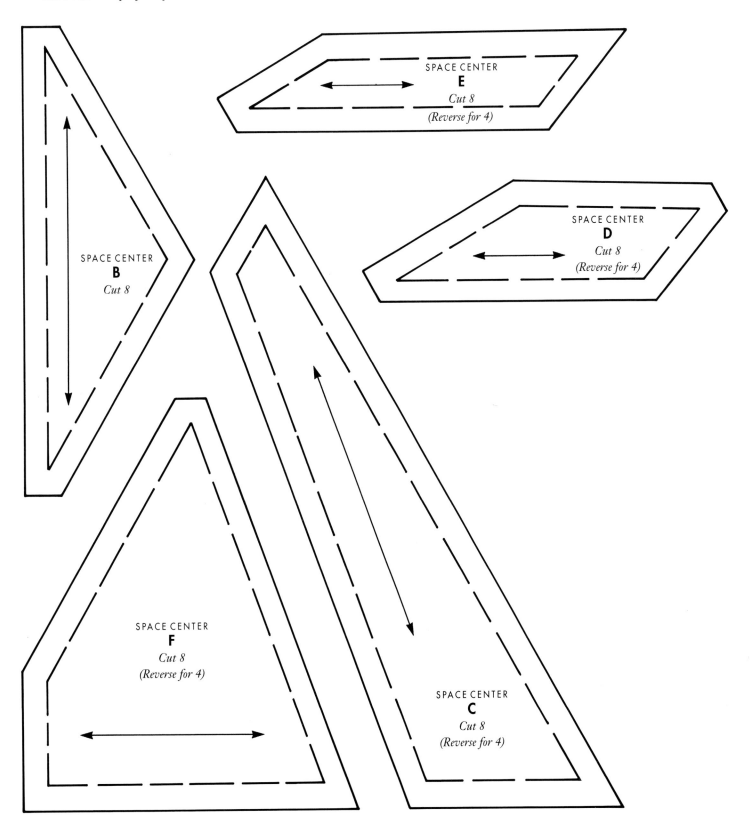

SPACE CENTER
E
Cut 8
(Reverse for 4)

SPACE CENTER
D
Cut 8
(Reverse for 4)

SPACE CENTER
B
Cut 8

SPACE CENTER
F
Cut 8
(Reverse for 4)

SPACE CENTER
C
Cut 8
(Reverse for 4)

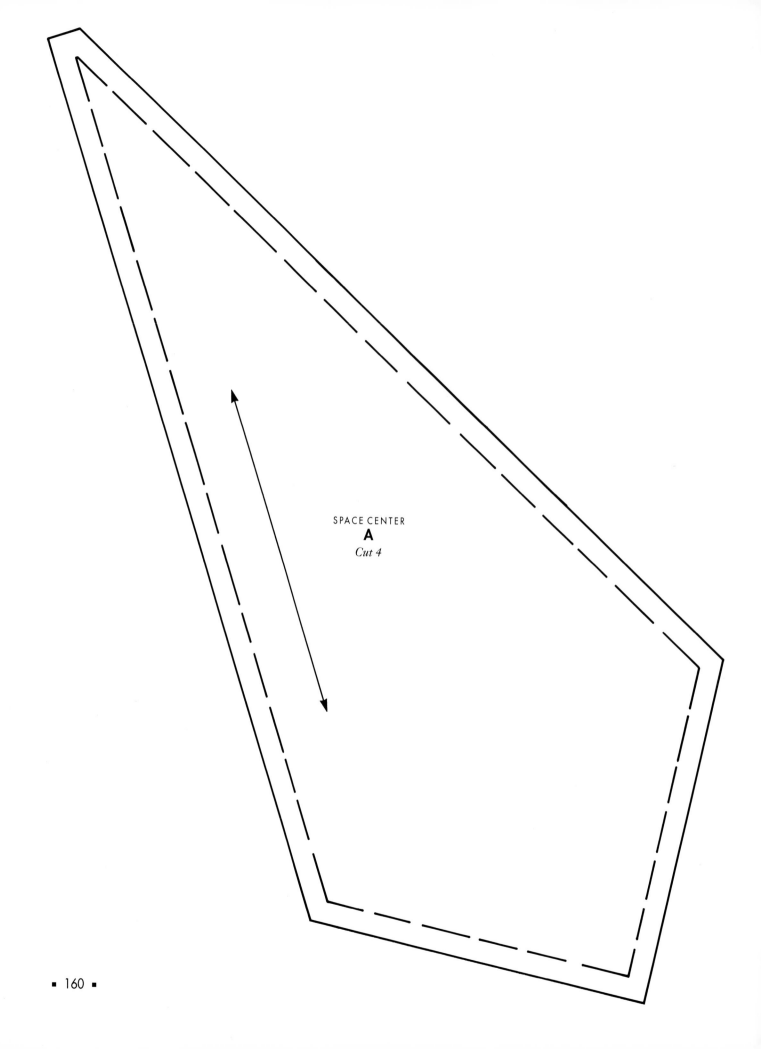

SPACE CENTER
A
Cut 4

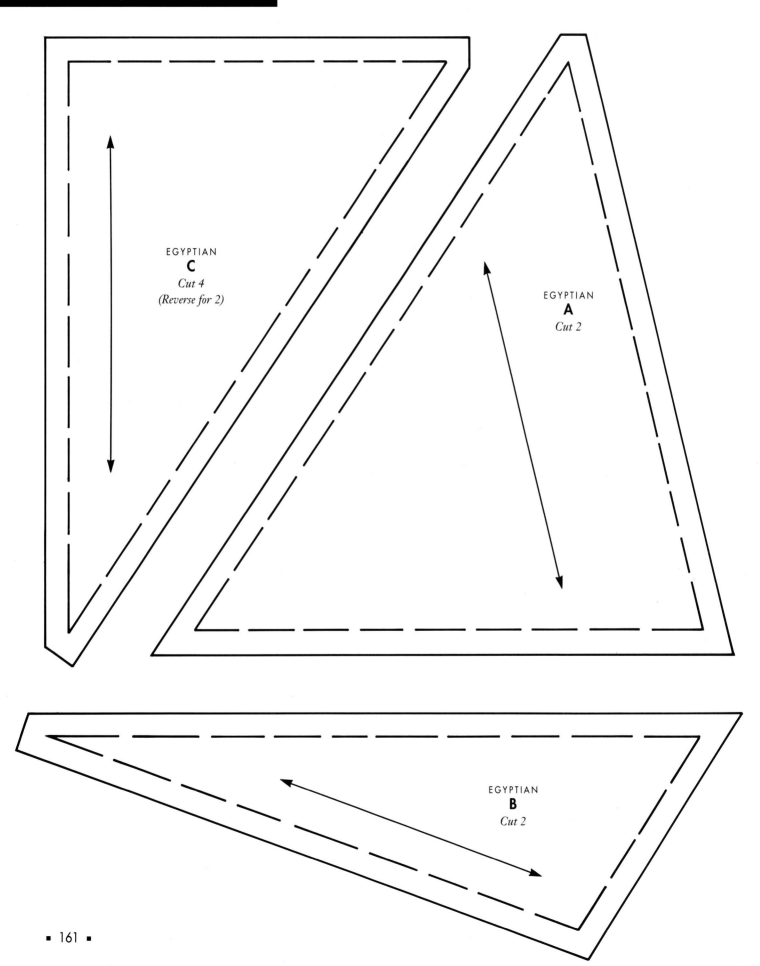

EGYPTIAN
C
Cut 4
(Reverse for 2)

EGYPTIAN
A
Cut 2

EGYPTIAN
B
Cut 2

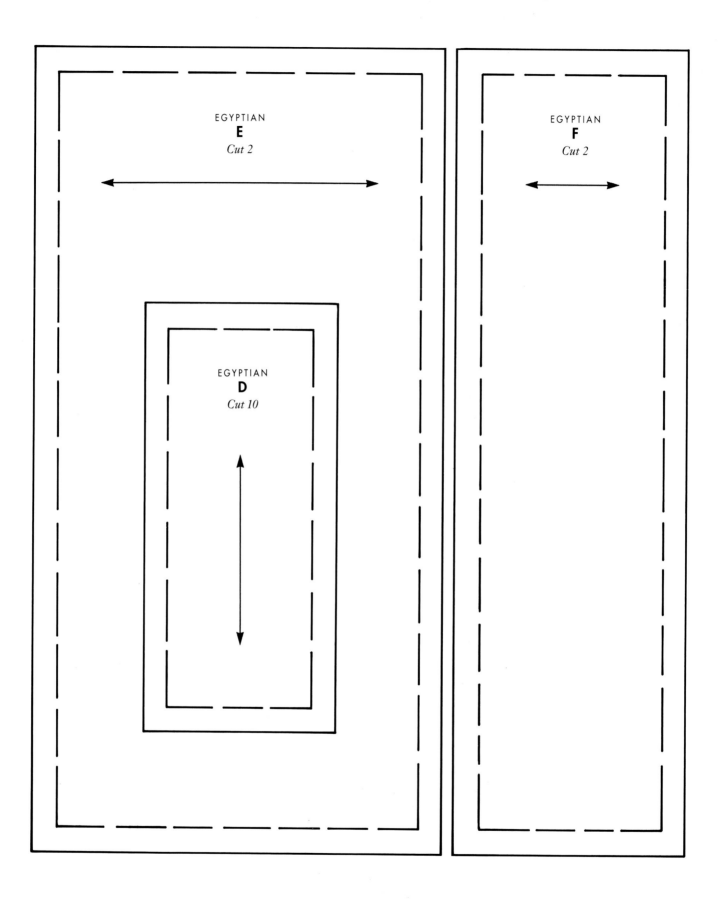

EGYPTIAN
E
Cut 2

EGYPTIAN
F
Cut 2

EGYPTIAN
D
Cut 10

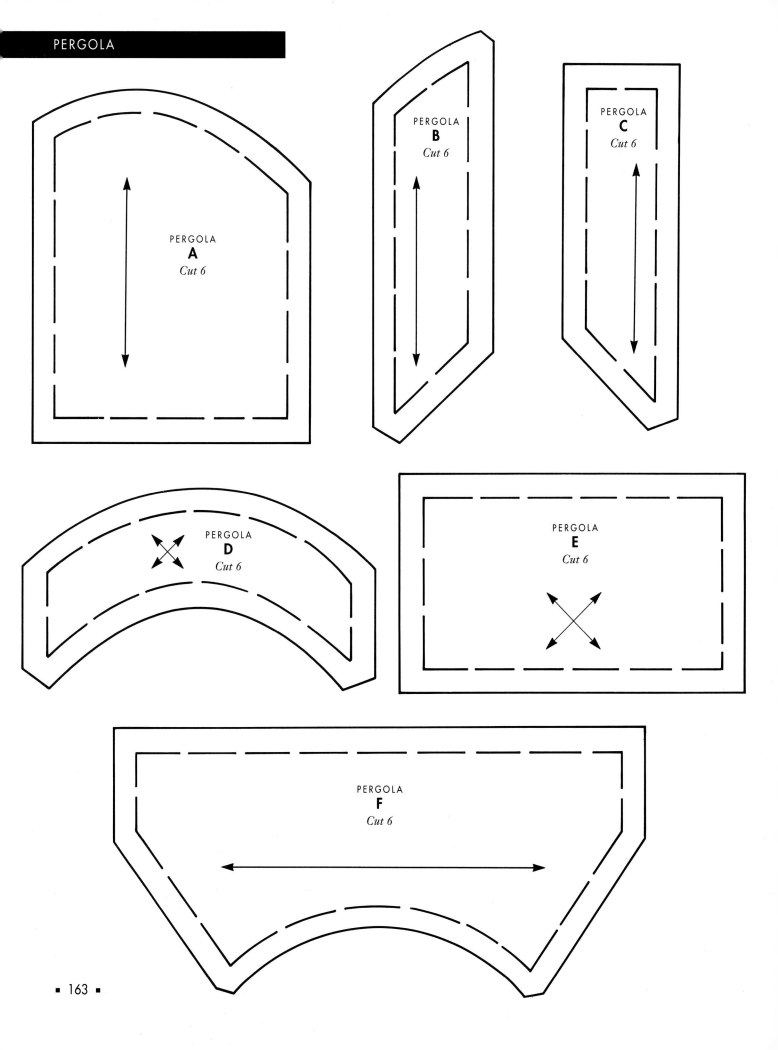

PERGOLA
A
Cut 6

PERGOLA
B
Cut 6

PERGOLA
C
Cut 6

PERGOLA
D
Cut 6

PERGOLA
E
Cut 6

PERGOLA
F
Cut 6

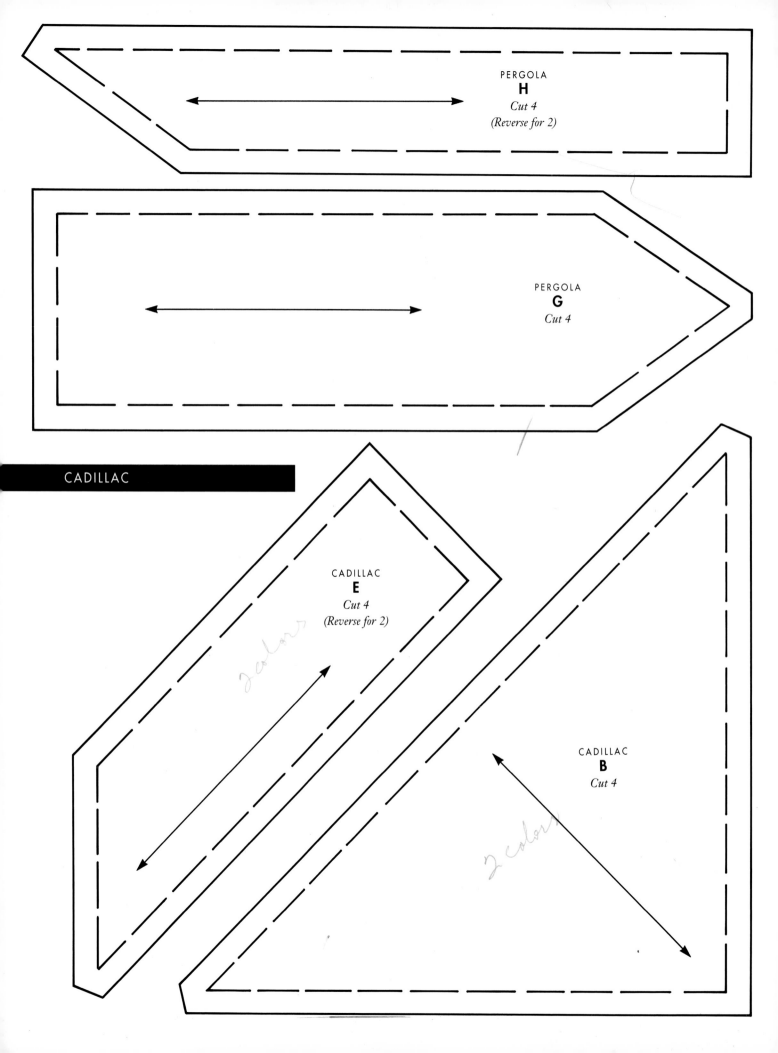

PERGOLA
H
Cut 4
(Reverse for 2)

PERGOLA
G
Cut 4

CADILLAC

CADILLAC
E
Cut 4
(Reverse for 2)

CADILLAC
B
Cut 4

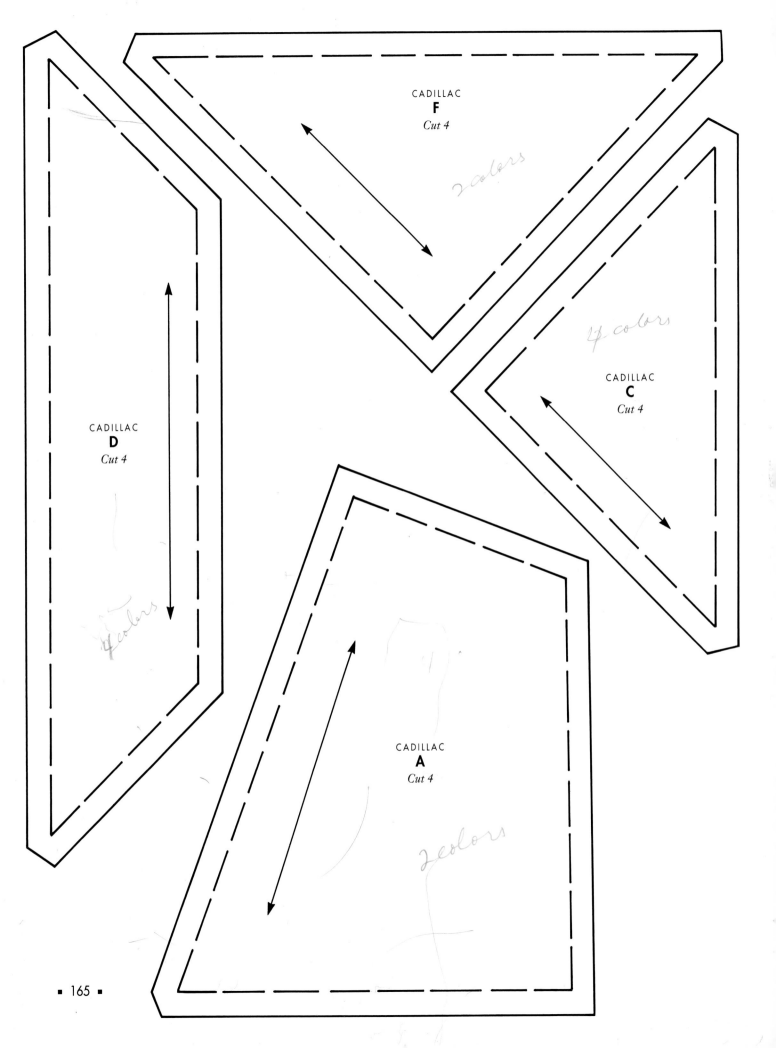

CADILLAC
F
Cut 4

2 colors

4 colors

CADILLAC
C
Cut 4

CADILLAC
D
Cut 4

4 colors

CADILLAC
A
Cut 4

2 colors

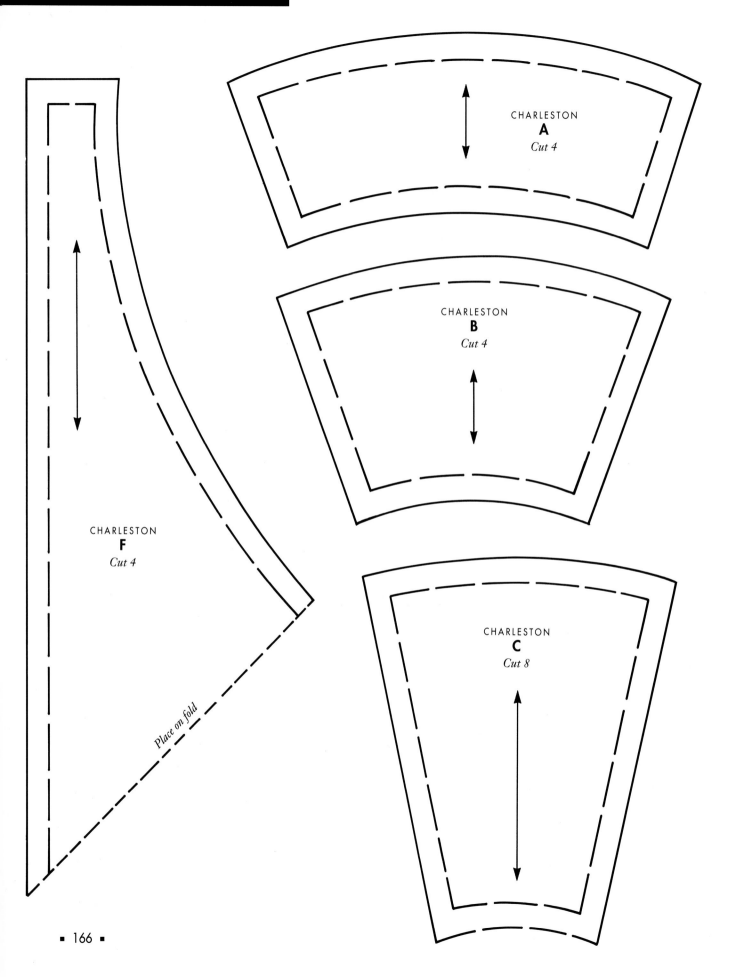

CHARLESTON
A
Cut 4

CHARLESTON
B
Cut 4

CHARLESTON
C
Cut 8

CHARLESTON
F
Cut 4

Place on fold

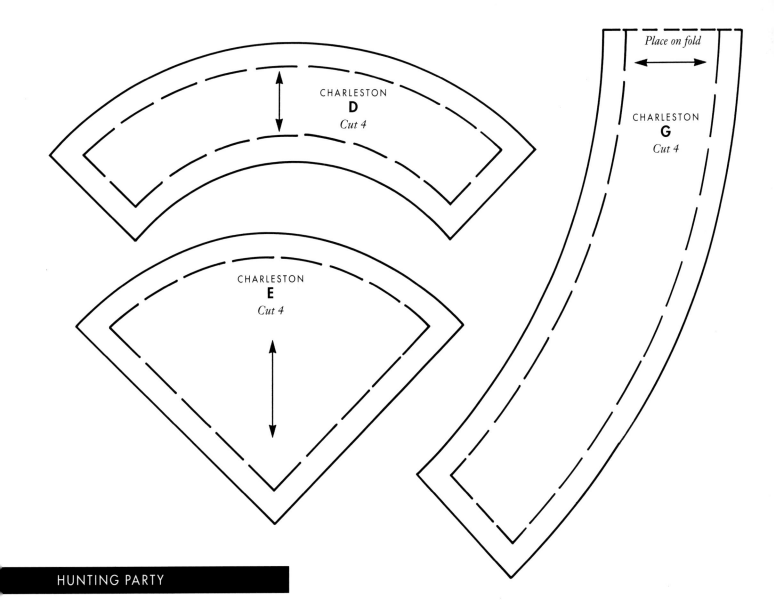

CHARLESTON
D
Cut 4

CHARLESTON
E
Cut 4

Place on fold

CHARLESTON
G
Cut 4

HUNTING PARTY

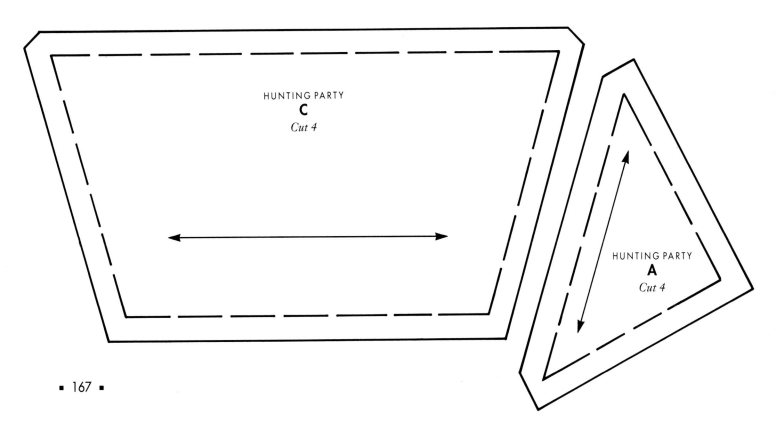

HUNTING PARTY
C
Cut 4

HUNTING PARTY
A
Cut 4

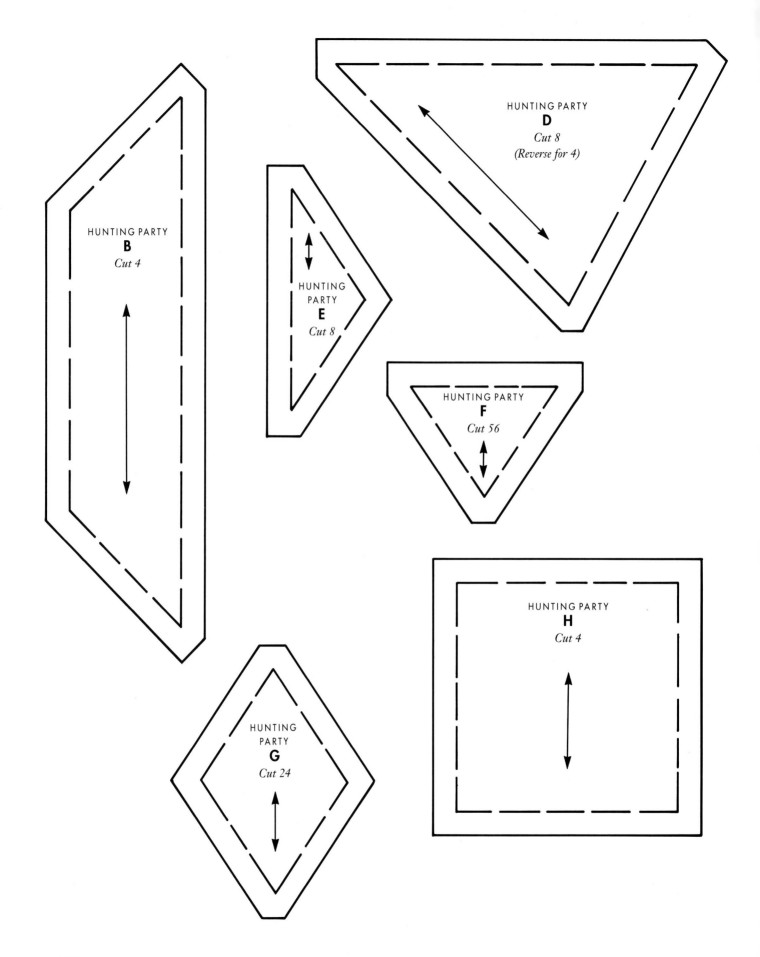

HUNTING PARTY
B
Cut 4

HUNTING PARTY
D
Cut 8
(Reverse for 4)

HUNTING
PARTY
E
Cut 8

HUNTING PARTY
F
Cut 56

HUNTING PARTY
H
Cut 4

HUNTING
PARTY
G
Cut 24

NOTE: *The templates indicate the number of pieces needed for making* **one block.** *To determine the number of pieces needed to make a complete quilt, refer to the cutting charts that accompany the quilt instructions.*

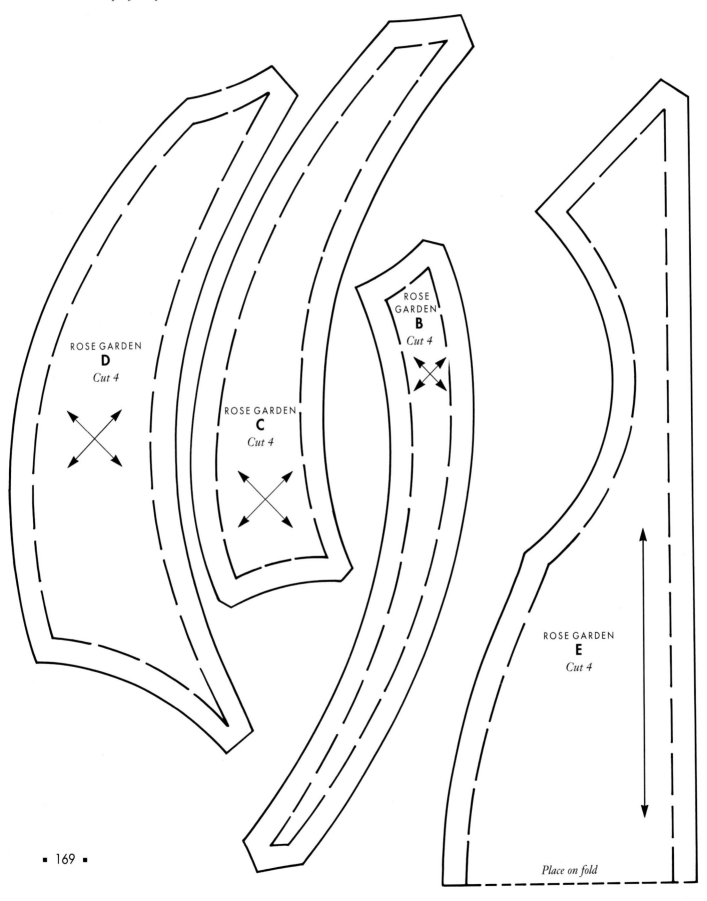

ROSE GARDEN
D
Cut 4

ROSE GARDEN
C
Cut 4

ROSE
GARDEN
B
Cut 4

ROSE GARDEN
E
Cut 4

Place on fold

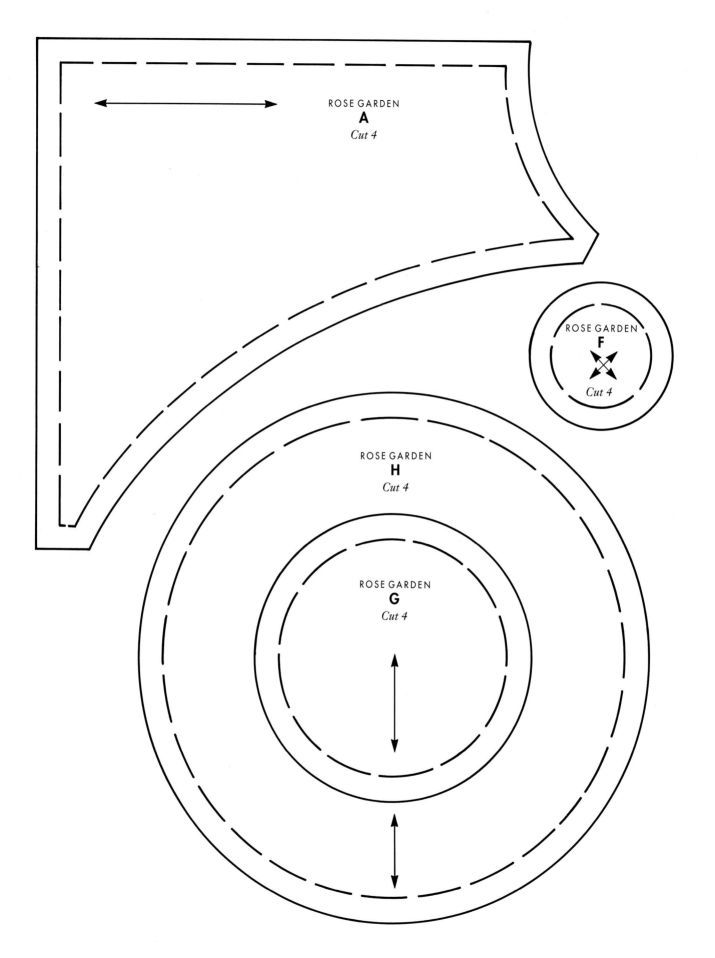

ROSE GARDEN
A
Cut 4

ROSE GARDEN
F
Cut 4

ROSE GARDEN
H
Cut 4

ROSE GARDEN
G
Cut 4

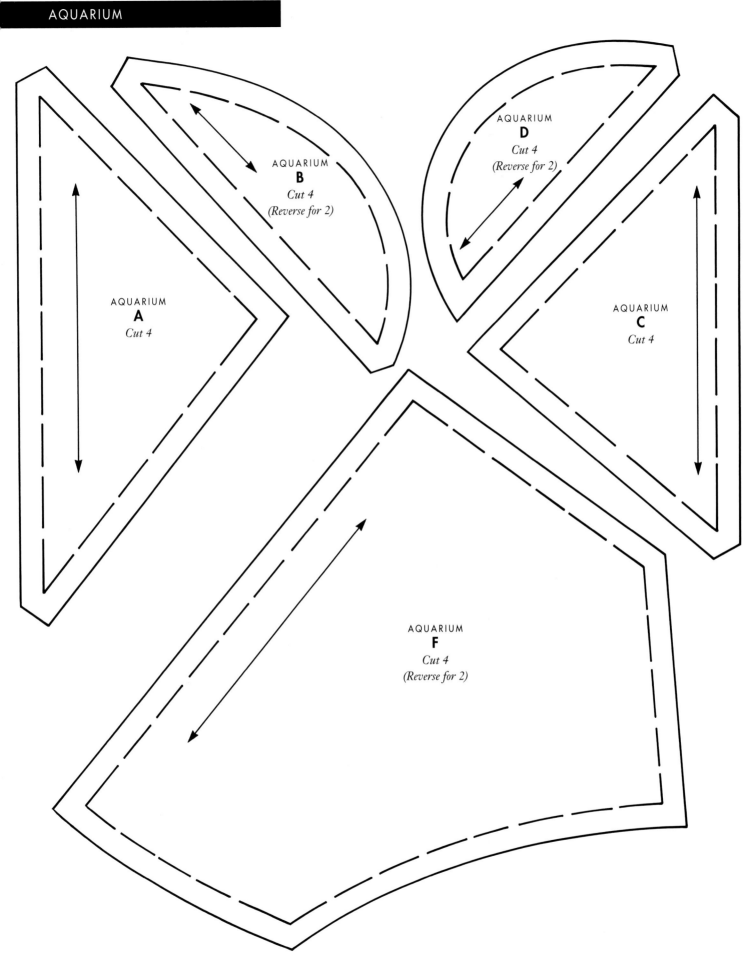

AQUARIUM
B
Cut 4
(Reverse for 2)

AQUARIUM
D
Cut 4
(Reverse for 2)

AQUARIUM
A
Cut 4

AQUARIUM
C
Cut 4

AQUARIUM
F
Cut 4
(Reverse for 2)

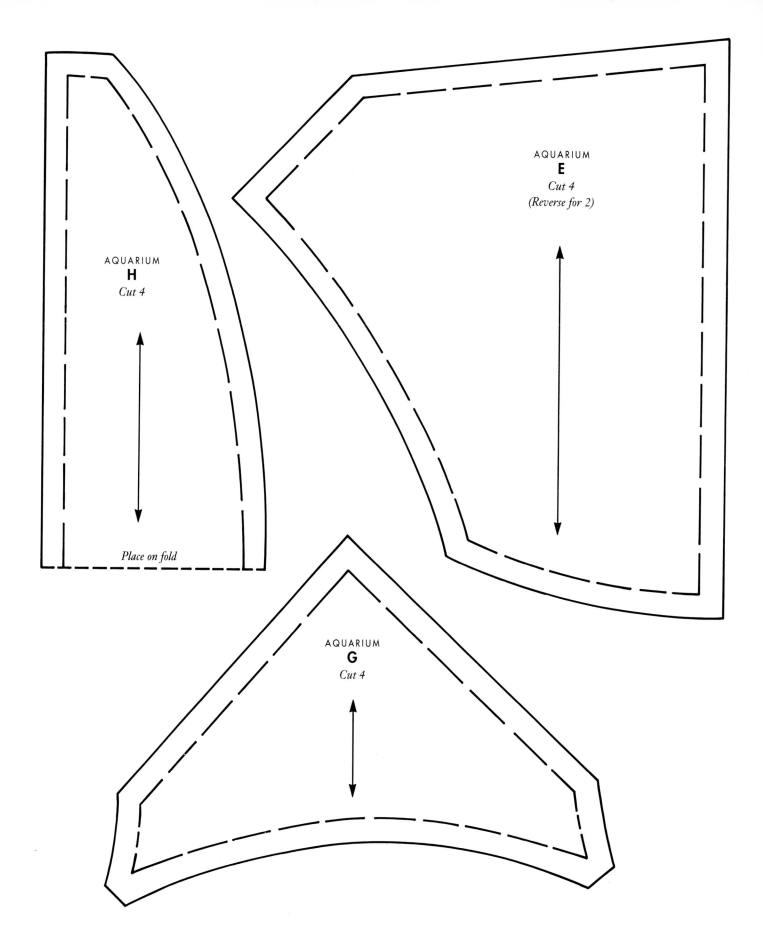

AQUARIUM
H
Cut 4

Place on fold

AQUARIUM
E
Cut 4
(Reverse for 2)

AQUARIUM
G
Cut 4

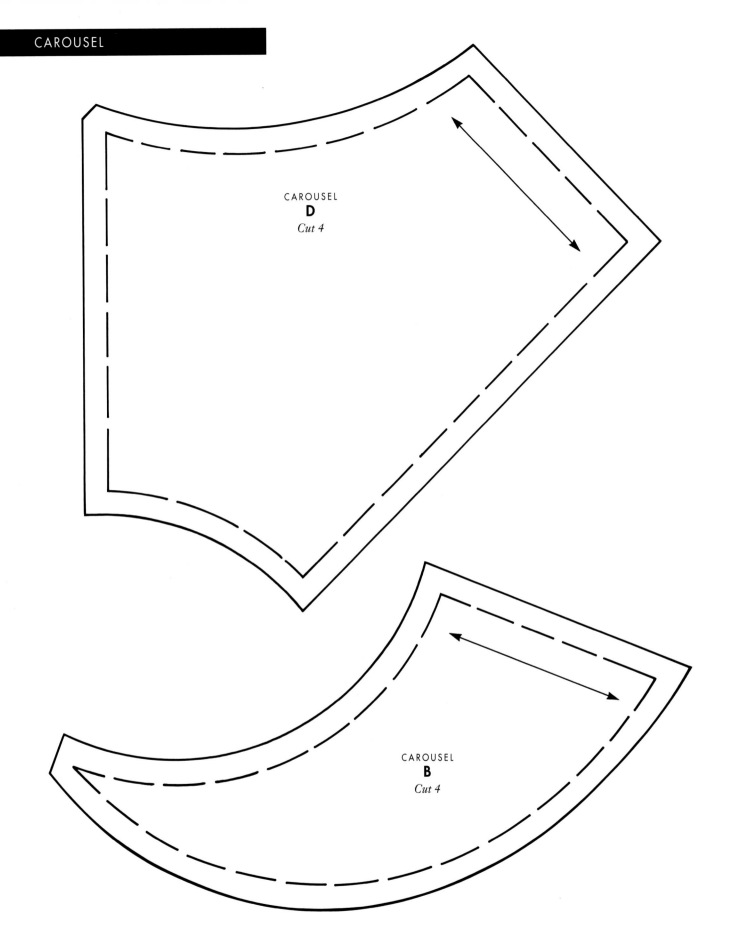

CAROUSEL
D
Cut 4

CAROUSEL
B
Cut 4

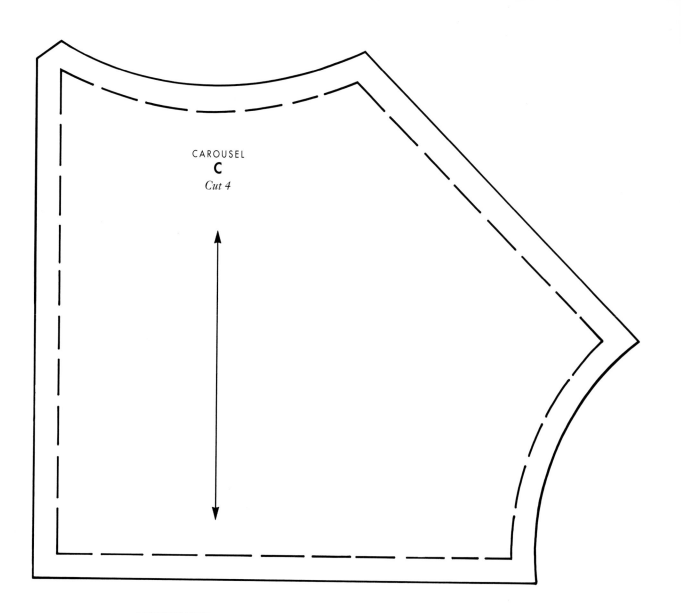

CAROUSEL
C
Cut 4

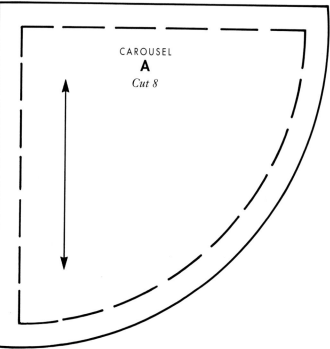

CAROUSEL
A
Cut 8

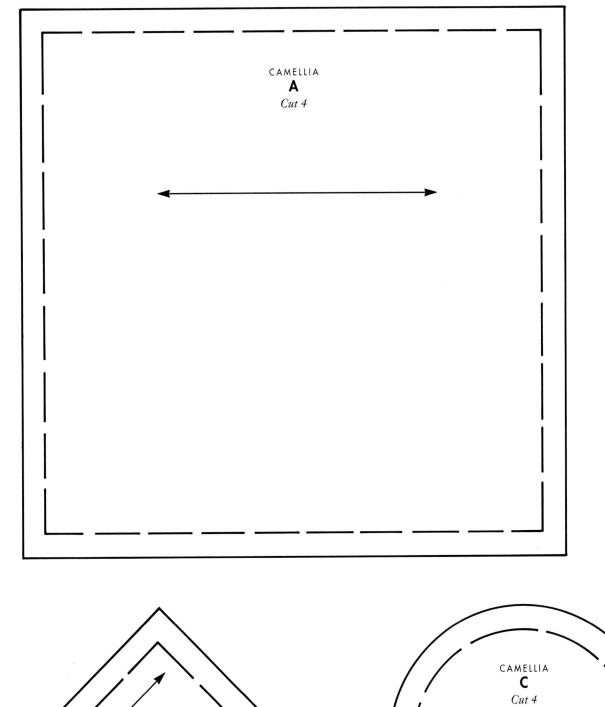

CAMELLIA
A
Cut 4

CAMELLIA
G
Cut 4

CAMELLIA
C
Cut 4

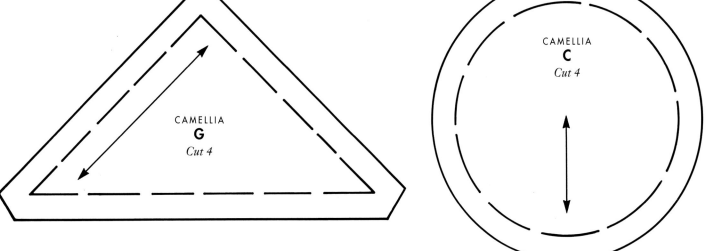

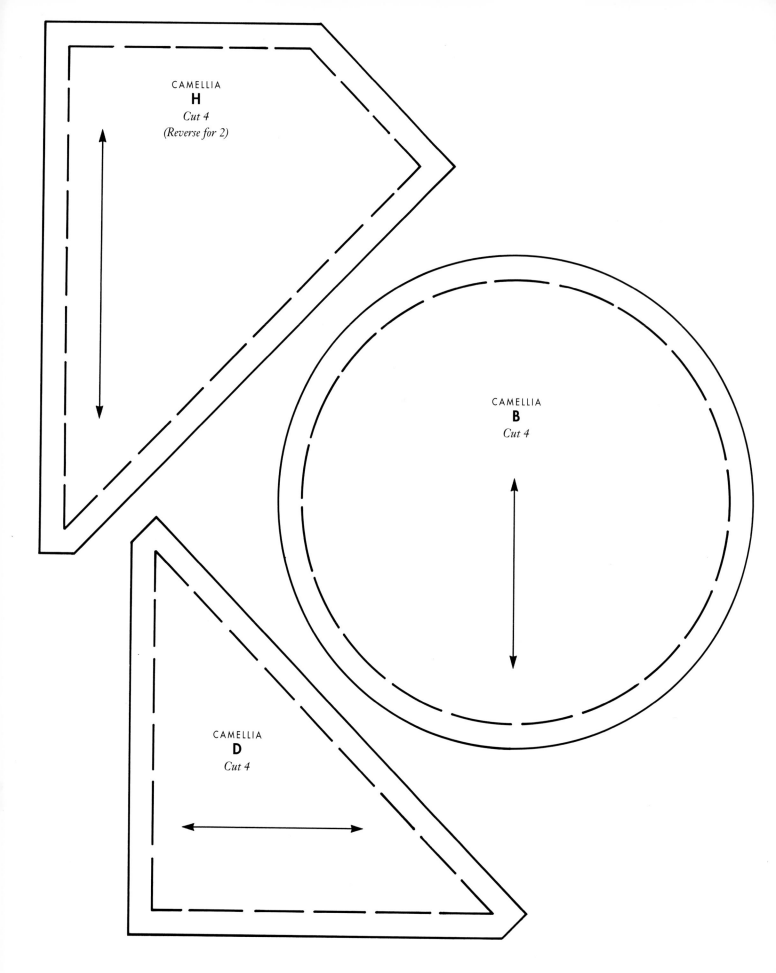

CAMELLIA
H
Cut 4
(Reverse for 2)

CAMELLIA
B
Cut 4

CAMELLIA
D
Cut 4

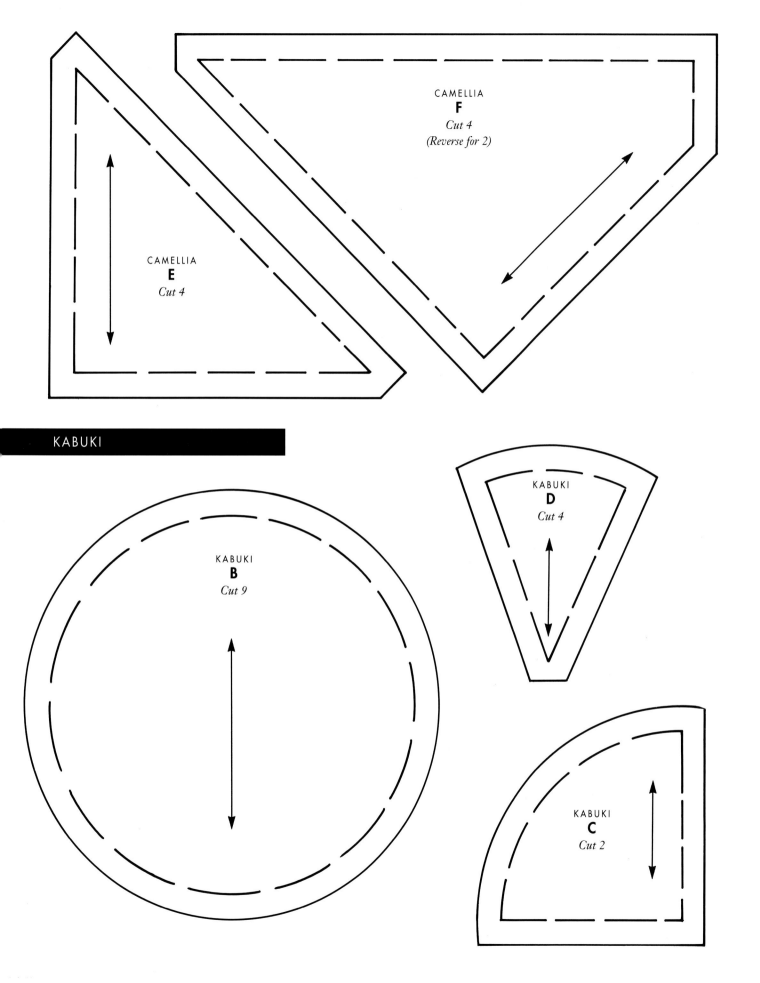

CAMELLIA
F
Cut 4
(Reverse for 2)

CAMELLIA
E
Cut 4

KABUKI

KABUKI
B
Cut 9

KABUKI
D
Cut 4

KABUKI
C
Cut 2

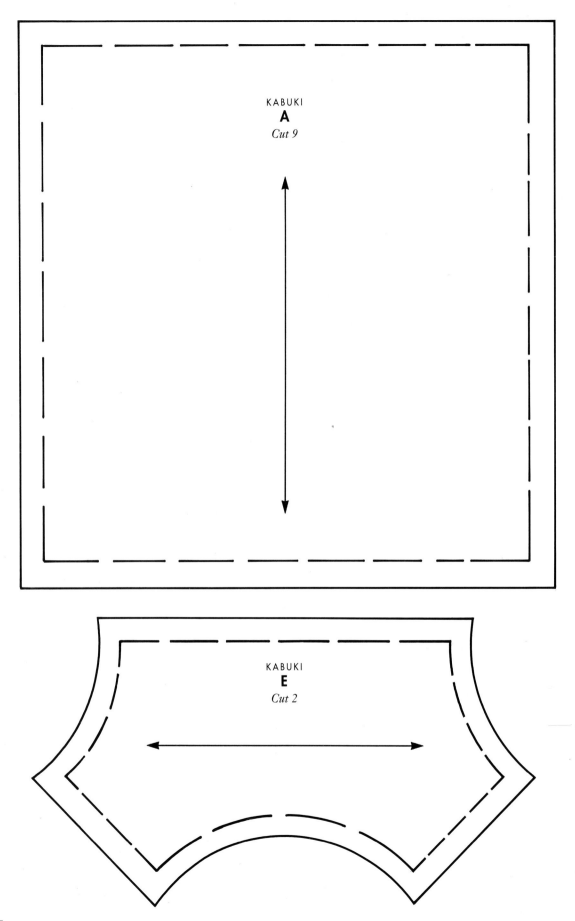

KABUKI
A
Cut 9

KABUKI
E
Cut 2

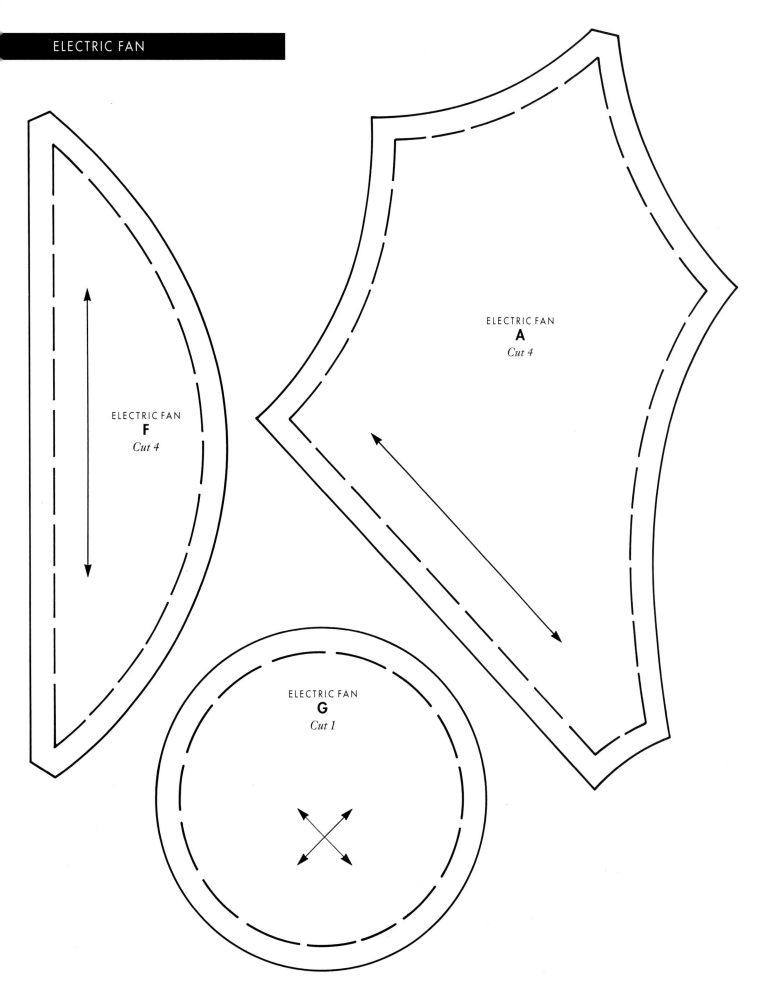

ELECTRIC FAN
F
Cut 4

ELECTRIC FAN
A
Cut 4

ELECTRIC FAN
G
Cut 1

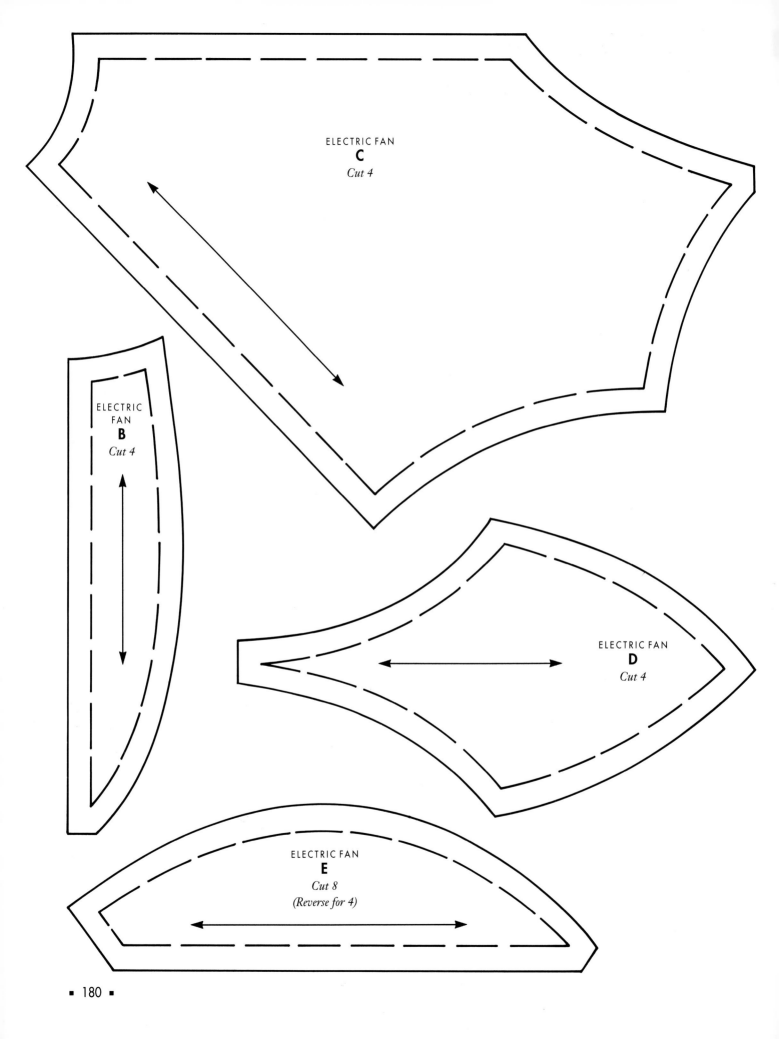

ELECTRIC FAN
C
Cut 4

ELECTRIC
FAN
B
Cut 4

ELECTRIC FAN
D
Cut 4

ELECTRIC FAN
E
Cut 8
(Reverse for 4)

NOTE: *The templates indicate the number of pieces needed for making* **one block.**
To determine the number of pieces needed to make a complete quilt, refer to the cutting charts that accompany the quilt instructions.

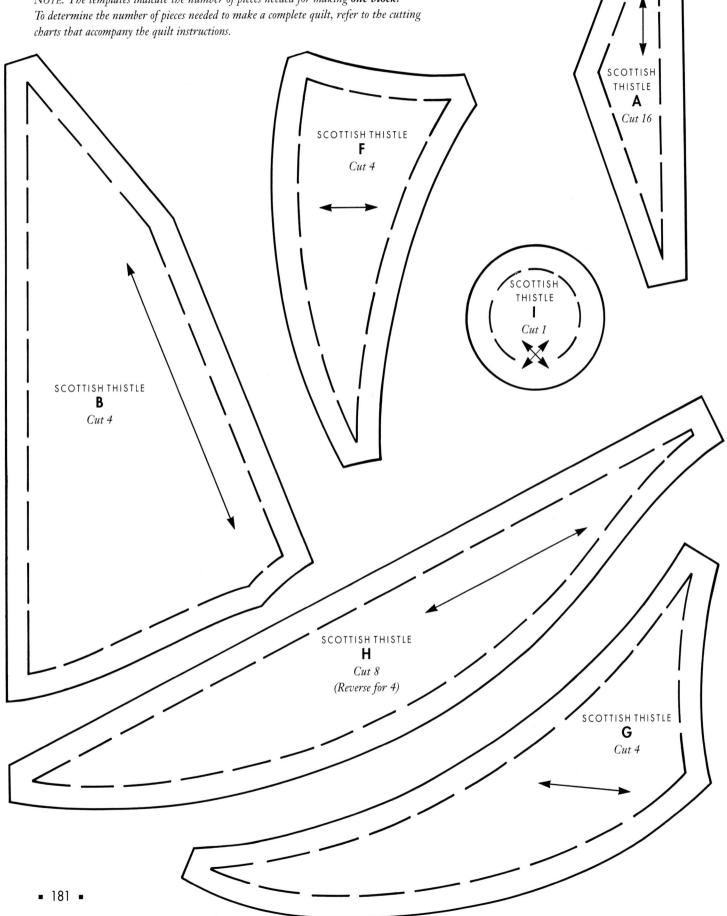

SCOTTISH THISTLE
A
Cut 16

SCOTTISH THISTLE
F
Cut 4

SCOTTISH
THISTLE
I
Cut 1

SCOTTISH THISTLE
B
Cut 4

SCOTTISH THISTLE
H
Cut 8
(Reverse for 4)

SCOTTISH THISTLE
G
Cut 4

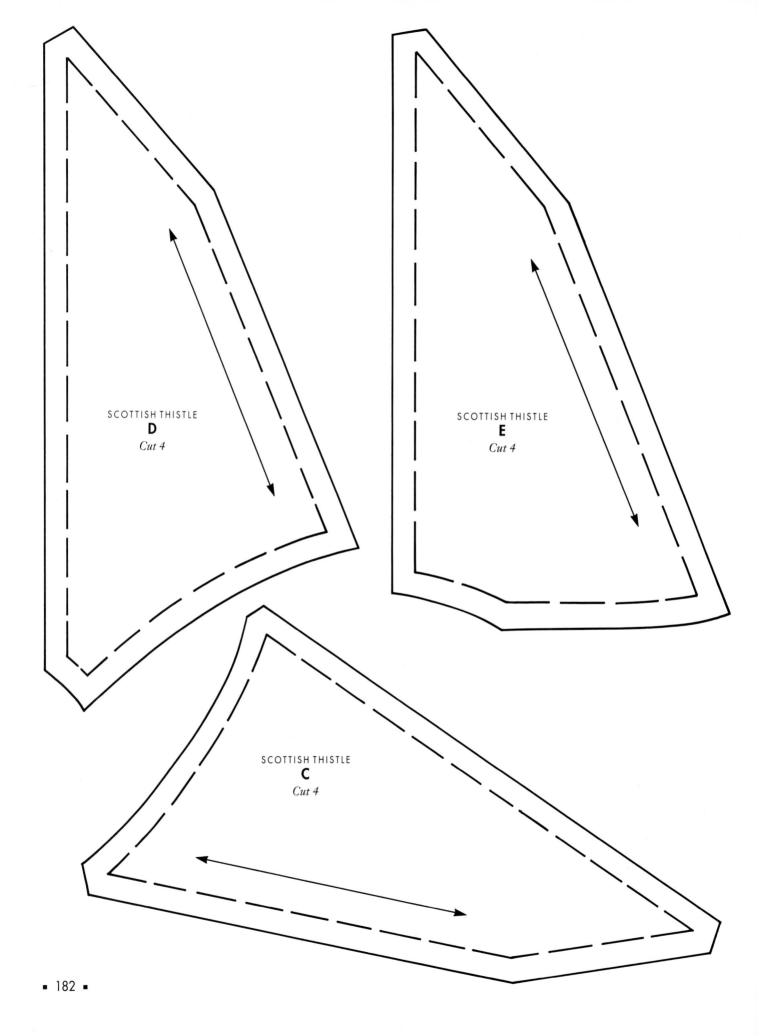

SCOTTISH THISTLE
D
Cut 4

SCOTTISH THISTLE
E
Cut 4

SCOTTISH THISTLE
C
Cut 4

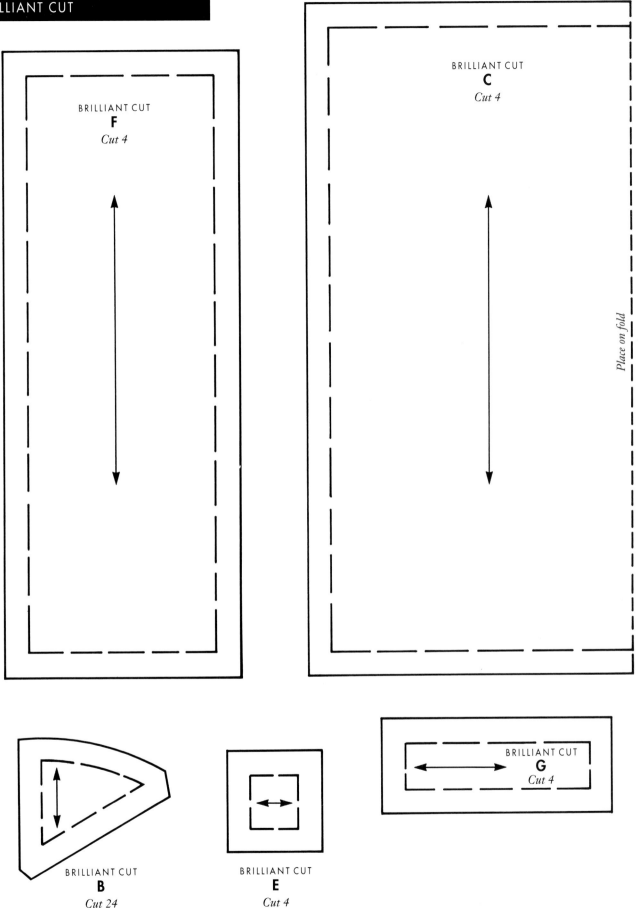

BRILLIANT CUT
F
Cut 4

BRILLIANT CUT
C
Cut 4

Place on fold

BRILLIANT CUT
B
Cut 24

BRILLIANT CUT
E
Cut 4

BRILLIANT CUT
G
Cut 4

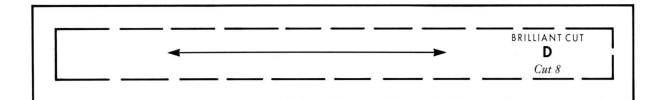

BRILLIANT CUT
D
Cut 8

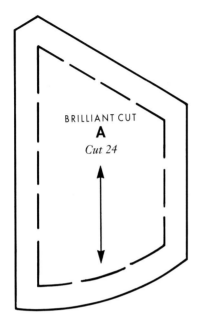

BRILLIANT CUT
A
Cut 24

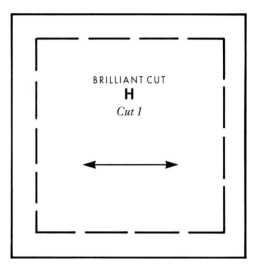

BRILLIANT CUT
H
Cut 1

O-SHOGATSU

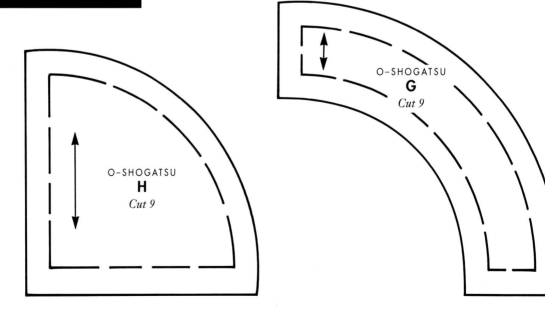

O-SHOGATSU
H
Cut 9

O-SHOGATSU
G
Cut 9

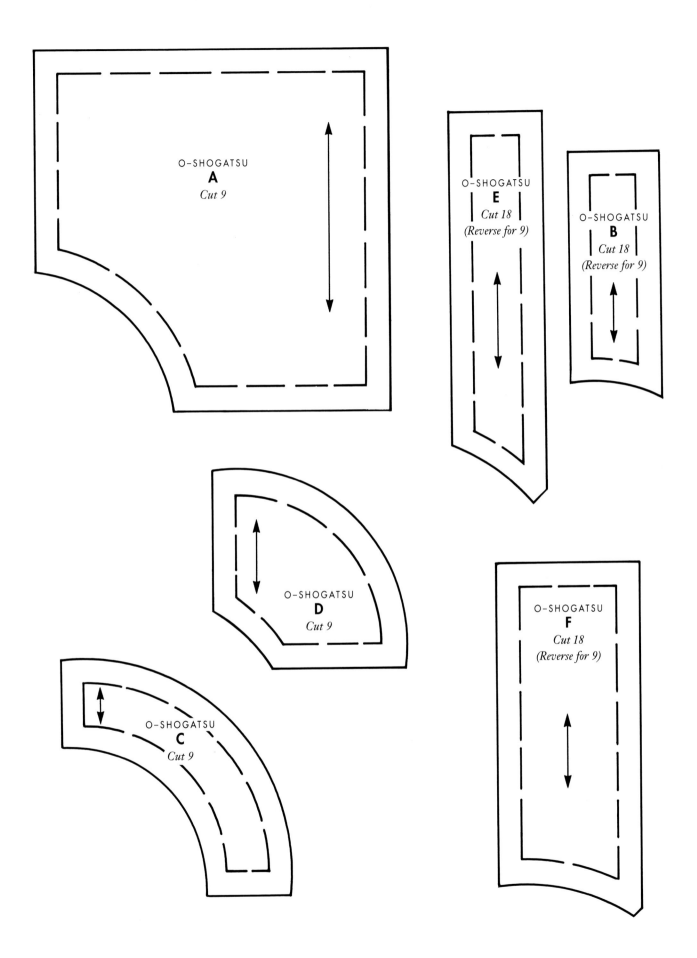

O-SHOGATSU
A
Cut 9

O-SHOGATSU
E
Cut 18
(Reverse for 9)

O-SHOGATSU
B
Cut 18
(Reverse for 9)

O-SHOGATSU
D
Cut 9

O-SHOGATSU
C
Cut 9

O-SHOGATSU
F
Cut 18
(Reverse for 9)

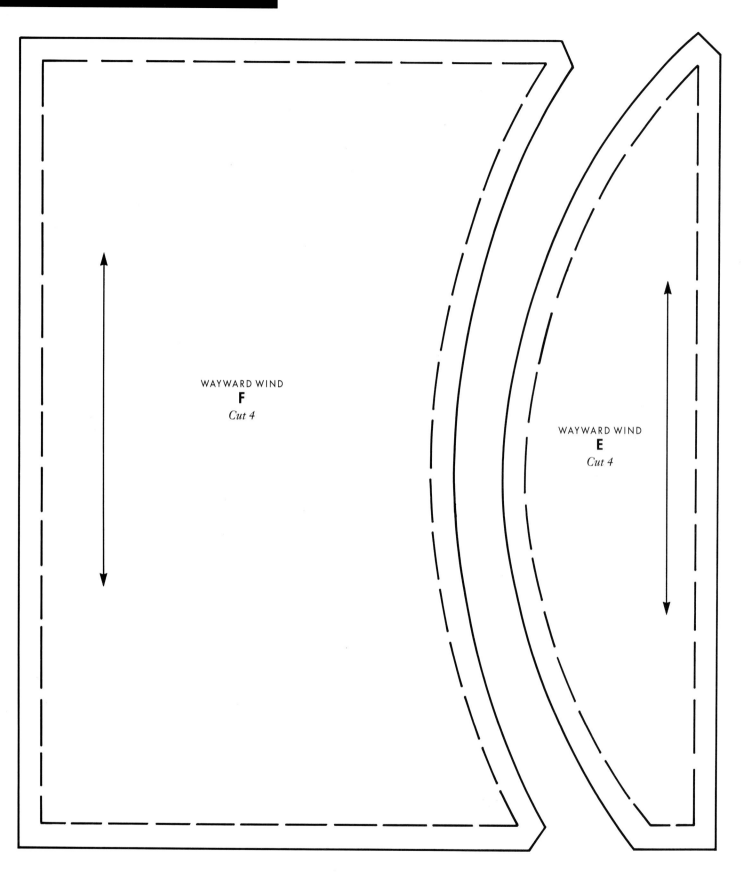

WAYWARD WIND
F
Cut 4

WAYWARD WIND
E
Cut 4

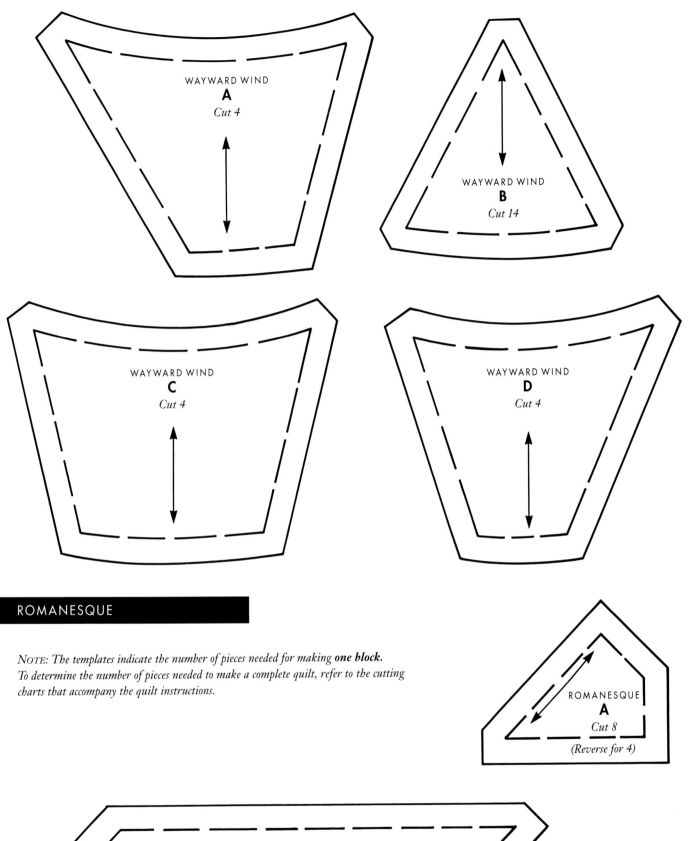

WAYWARD WIND
A
Cut 4

WAYWARD WIND
B
Cut 14

WAYWARD WIND
C
Cut 4

WAYWARD WIND
D
Cut 4

ROMANESQUE

NOTE: *The templates indicate the number of pieces needed for making* **one block.** *To determine the number of pieces needed to make a complete quilt, refer to the cutting charts that accompany the quilt instructions.*

ROMANESQUE
A
Cut 8
(Reverse for 4)

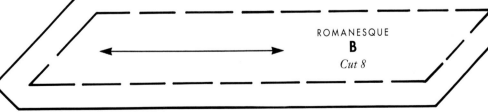

ROMANESQUE
B
Cut 8

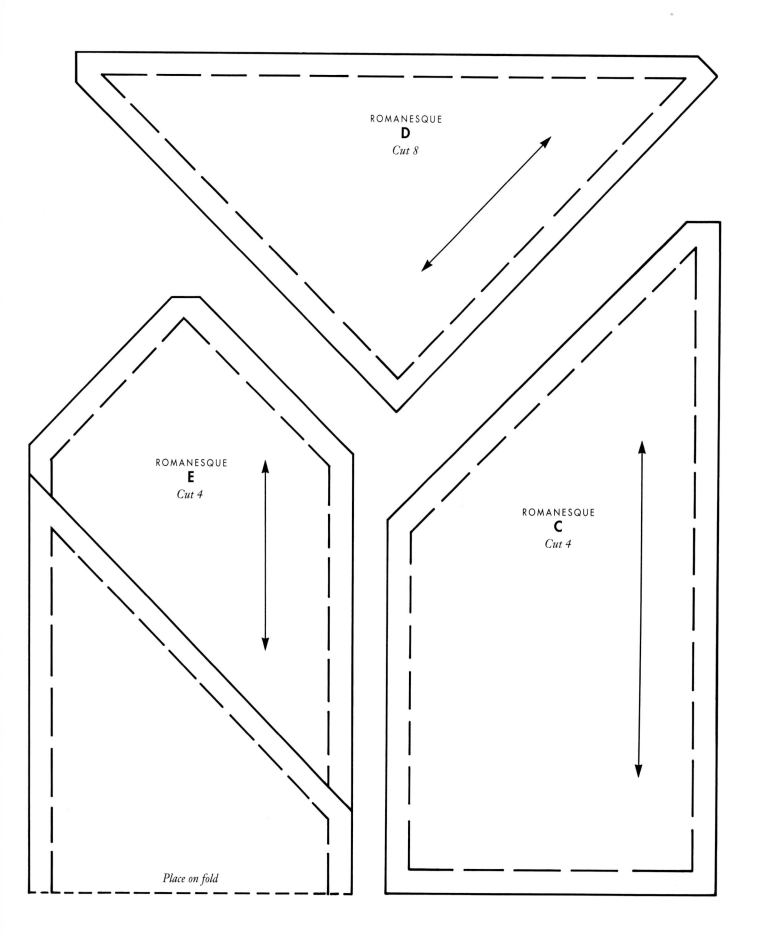

ROMANESQUE
D
Cut 8

ROMANESQUE
E
Cut 4

Place on fold

ROMANESQUE
C
Cut 4

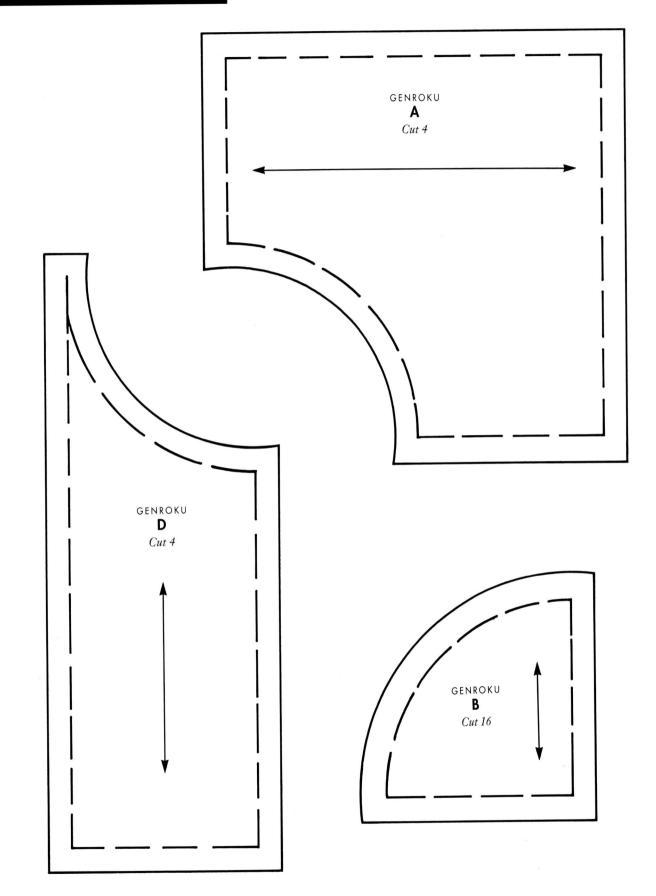

GENROKU
A
Cut 4

GENROKU
D
Cut 4

GENROKU
B
Cut 16

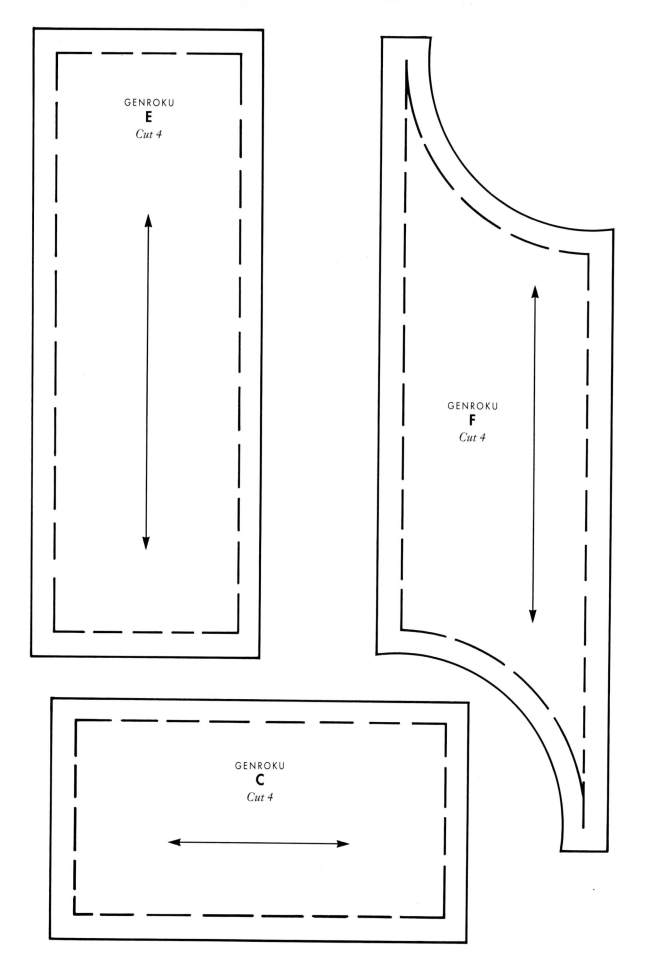

GENROKU
E
Cut 4

GENROKU
F
Cut 4

GENROKU
C
Cut 4

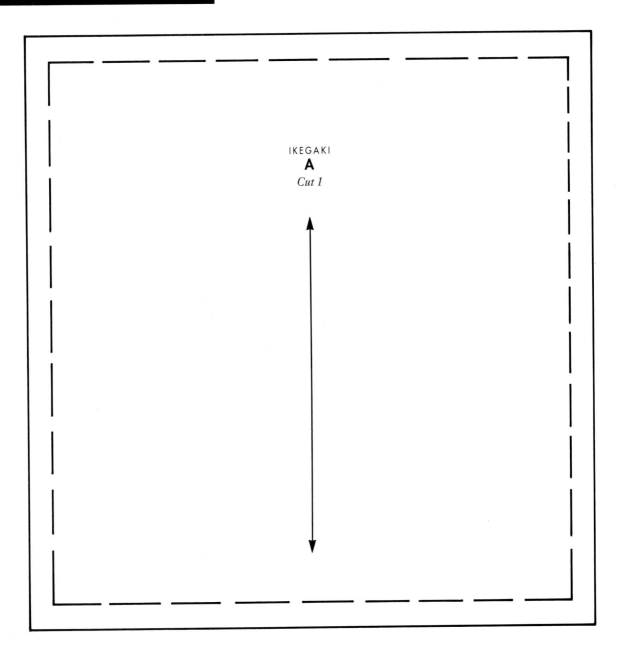

IKEGAKI
A
Cut 1

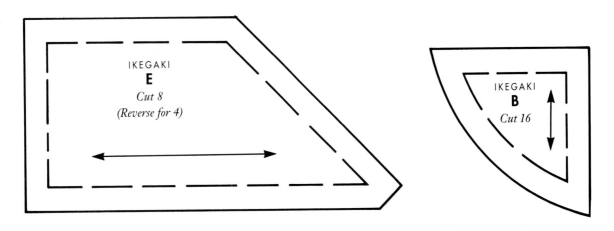

IKEGAKI
E
Cut 8
(Reverse for 4)

IKEGAKI
B
Cut 16

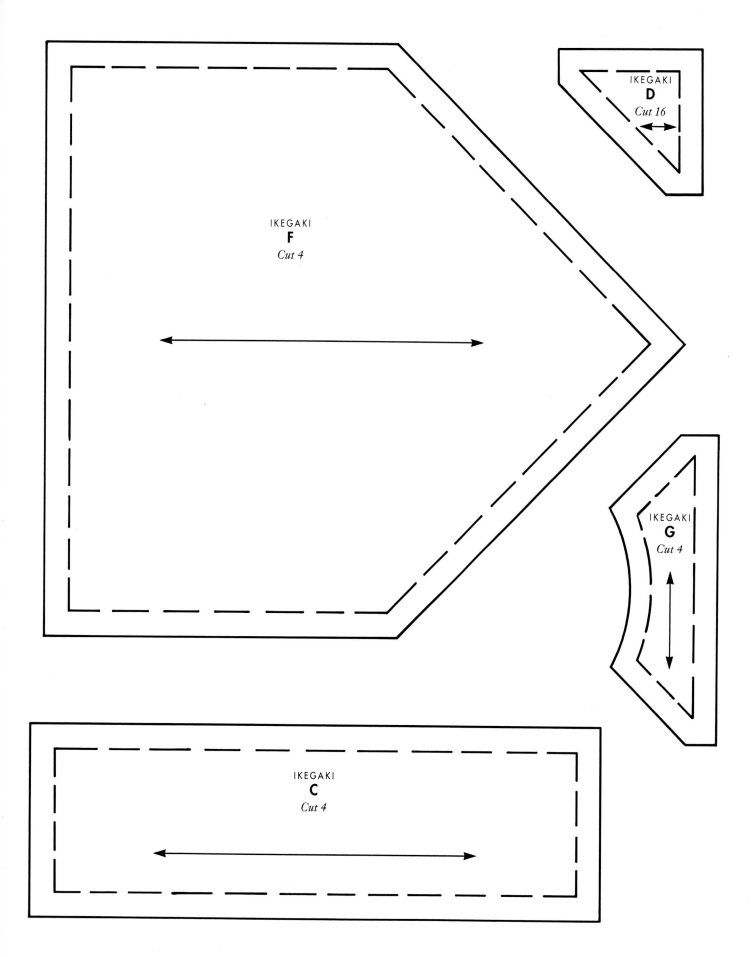

IKEGAKI
D
Cut 16

IKEGAKI
F
Cut 4

IKEGAKI
G
Cut 4

IKEGAKI
C
Cut 4

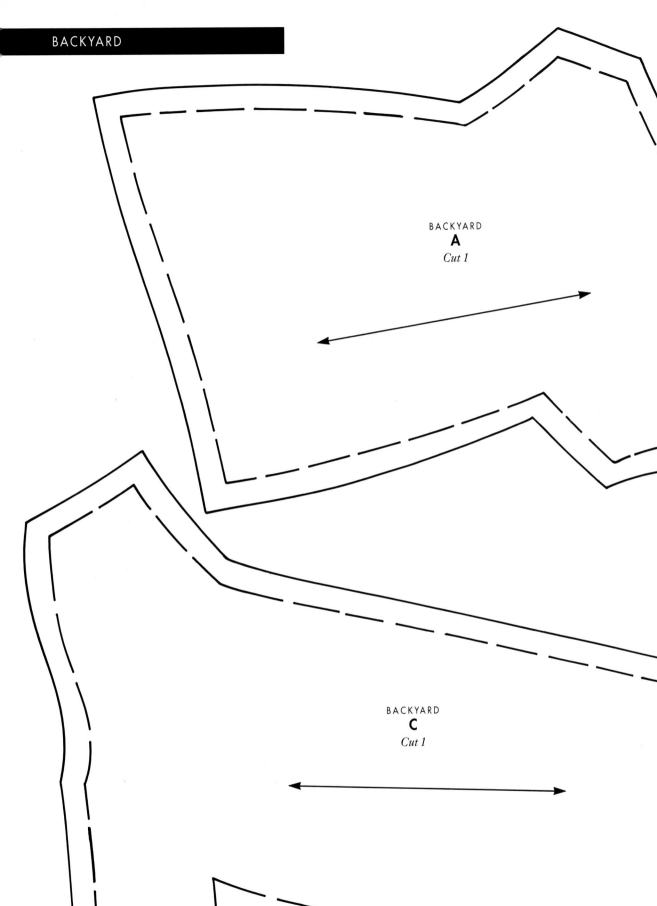

BACKYARD
A
Cut 1

BACKYARD
C
Cut 1

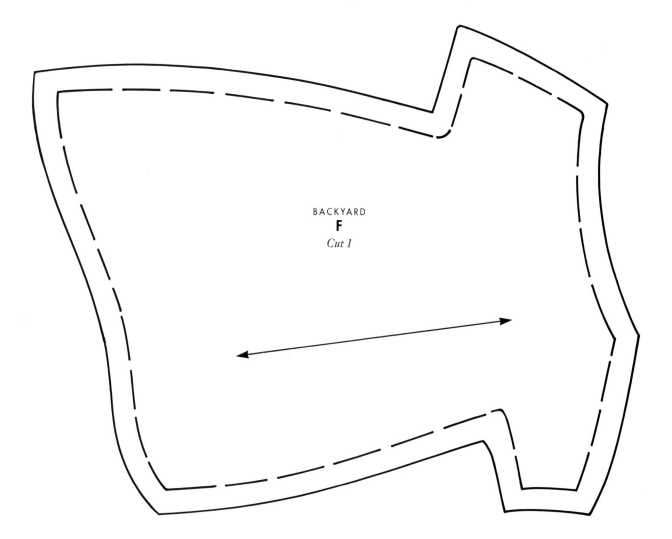

BACKYARD
F
Cut 1

BACKYARD
G
(Background piece)
Cut 1
16½" × 16½" (42cm × 42cm)
Includes ¼" (6mm) seam allowance

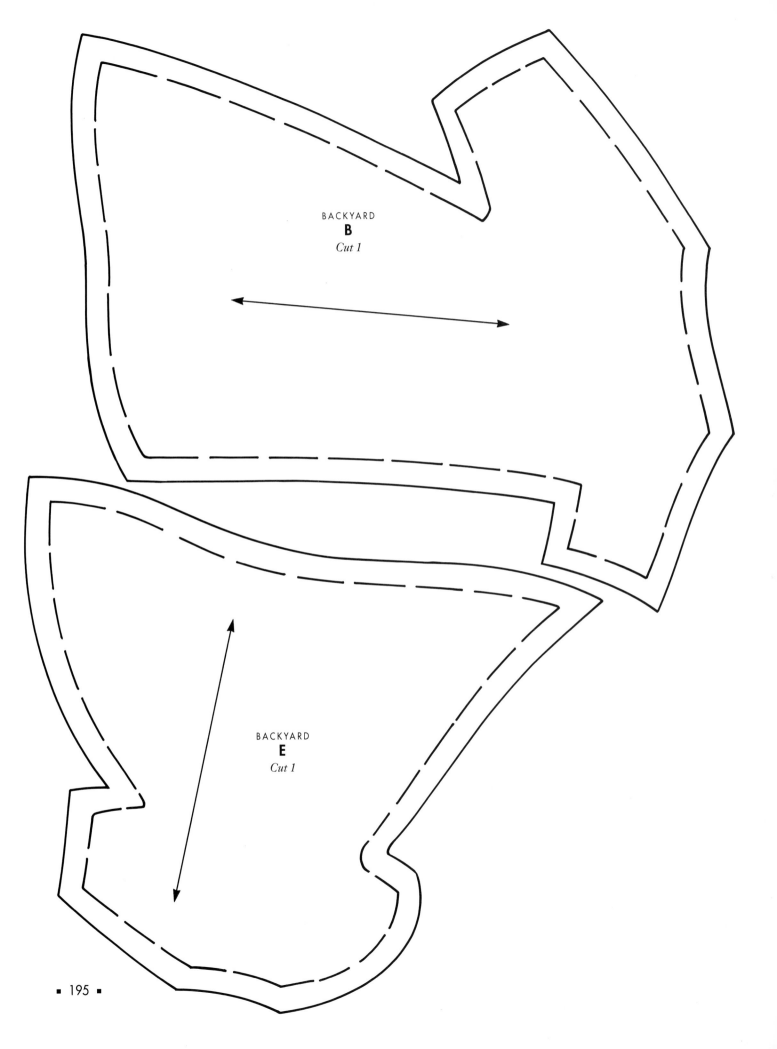

BACKYARD
B
Cut 1

BACKYARD
E
Cut 1

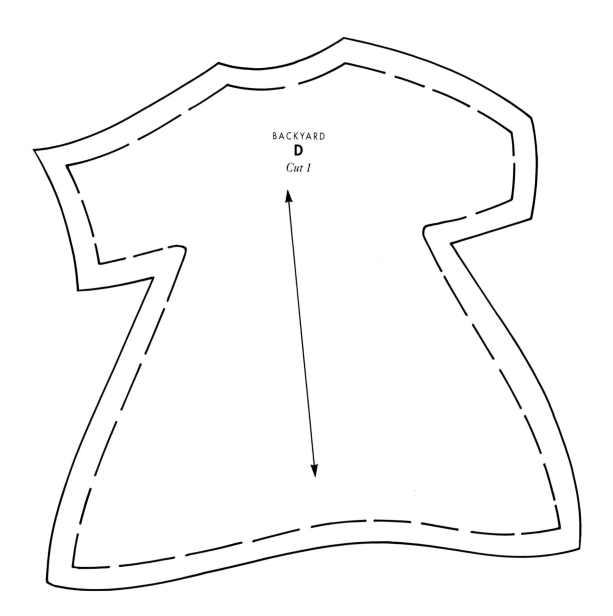

BACKYARD
D
Cut 1

LESSON PLANS

Suggestions for a One-Day Workshop
Making a Simple Block: Quattrocentro

(FOR BEGINNING AND INTERMEDIATE QUILTERS)

During this sample lesson, students will make one of the easier blocks in this book. The process includes learning to enlarge a diagram to an actual-size pattern, learning and practicing a precise method of hand-piecing, and looking at color and pattern in fabrics in a new way.

FIRST HOUR: Give each student one or more photocopies of the diagram for the block (page 39). Discuss color selection and placement in the block: contrast of light and dark colors, texture, movement, and use of bold fabrics with large designs. Instruct students to color their diagrams to experiment with colors of their choosing and then to make their final decision as to the colors they will use.

SECOND HOUR: Students draw the actual-size pattern for the block on white paper, label each piece, and cut out each one (these do not include seam allowance). Students then make templates for the block, using the patterns on page 126 (these do include seam allowance).

THIRD HOUR: After discussing the type of fabric to be used for the project, students select the fabrics that they will need to

SUPPLY LIST

Sewing and quilting needles
Sewing and quilting thread
Straight pins
Paper and fabric scissors
Tracing paper
Ruler
Pencil
Colored pencils
Thimble
Fabric marker (or pencil)
White drawing paper
Notebook
Fabric for piecing the quilt top
Backing fabric
Batting

match their color sketches as closely as possible. They cut the fabric pieces using the templates, following the lengthwise grain or the print of the patterns.

FOURTH AND FIFTH HOURS: Students lay the pattern pieces (without seam allowance) on the fabric pieces and draw around the edges with the fabric marker or pencil, indicating the seamline. They pin and sew together the pieces to be joined and iron them flat. I then have them check, using the pattern pieces, that the sewn fabric pieces are the correct size before going on to the next piece.

SIXTH HOUR: After completing the block top following the instructions and diagrams on page 42, students join the top, batting, and quilt backing with basting stitches. Students may quilt in freeform designs or following the seamlines.

Suggestions for an Extended Classroom Schedule Making a More Complex Design: Tropical Garden *Block or Quilt*

(FOR INTERMEDIATE AND ADVANCED QUILTERS)

These are ideas to be incorporated into a course for teaching experienced quilters how to refine their piecing, quilting, and appliqué skills. The course is based on a design that includes many curved seams, which are more difficult than straight seams but which offer more design possibilities. It also includes suggestions for those who wish to encourage students to create their own *Tropical Garden* flower-based designs. Feel free to use these ideas along with your own teaching experience to modify the course as you wish.

Using the *Tropical Garden* design on page 63, begin by instructing students to make the block following the procedure outlined in the earlier lessons. (Students may make and finish one block or a complete quilt.)

During the piecing stage, demonstrate the type of appliqué technique used in this design; you may want to demonstrate

SUPPLY LIST

Sewing and quilting needles
Sewing and quilting thread
Straight pins
Paper and fabric scissors
Tracing paper
Ruler
Pencil
Colored pencils
Thimble
Fabric marker (or pencil)
White drawing paper
Notebook
Fabric for piecing the quilt top
Backing fabric
Batting

other techniques for piecing curved seams and other forms of appliqué as well.

Discuss the use of color in the project — the colors in the *Tropical Garden* quilt shown in this book are very brilliant, and to get a similar feeling, students should choose fabrics in summer patterns with bright and bold prints.

To encourage creativity, demonstrate how new flower petal designs can be drawn. Students who have completed the *Tropical Garden* block shown in this book may wish to progress toward creating their own *Tropical Garden* designs. Instruct students to make freehand drawings and fill in the areas using colored pencils.

Students who have created new designs can form small groups and share their ideas concerning new designs and patterns. In addition, you can conduct an open discussion with students about the pros and cons of each design.

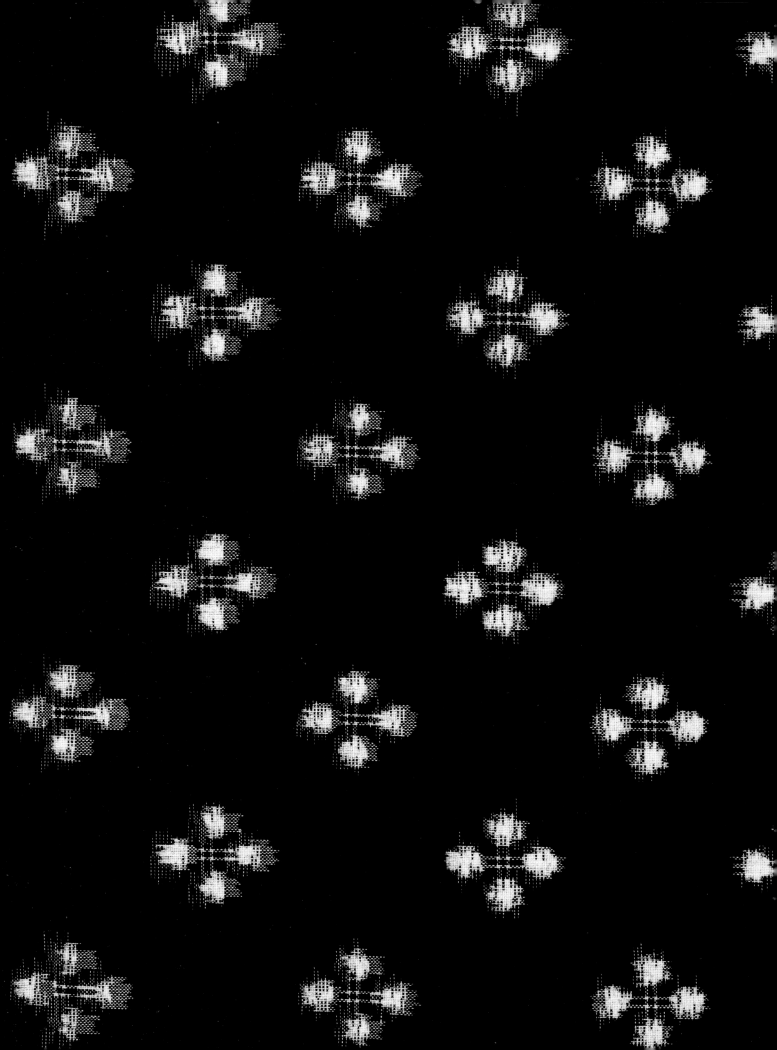